FAMILY SPAIN

FAMILY SPAIN

FRANK BARRETT

B🍃XTREE

First published in Great Britain in 1994 by Boxtree Limited

Text © copyright Frank Barrett 1994

The right of Frank Barrett to be identified as Author of this Work has
been asserted by him in accordance with the Copyright, Designs and
Patents Act 1988.

10 9 8 7 6 5 4 3 2 1

Printed in Great Britain by The Bath Press, Avon

Boxtree Limited
Broadwall House
21 Broadwall
London SE1 9PL

A CIP catalogue entry for this book is available from the British Library

ISBN 0 7522 1622 8

Designed by Blackjacks, London

Cover design by Robert Updegraff

Front cover photograph courtesy of Tony Stone Images

CONTENTS

FOREWORD

Spain is certainly *the* family holiday destination for the majority of British travellers. When we think of sun and sand destinations we inevitably think first of the Spanish Costas, the Balearic Island of Majorca and, in winter, the Canary Islands.

Stand in Gatwick's main departures hall on a busy August Saturday and every other holidaymaker will be heading off to some Spanish resort: Spain now accounts for half of the inclusive package market. The British love affair with Spain has suffered ups and downs. Other destinations have attempted to woo the British with the promise of lower prices: customers are encouraged to experiment with the Algarve, the Greek Islands, Tunisia and Turkey – but inevitably Spain draws them back. The country offers guaranteed value for money with facilities and an ambience familiar to the British visitor.

From this bedrock of popularity, Spain is now attempting to attract visitors to less well-known parts of the country: to its cultural sights, its ancient cities, its splendid old hotels, its breathtaking national parks, its unspoilt coastline to the north.

For families who enjoy French *gites* and Italian farmhouses, Spain is probably a pleasure yet to be discovered. A few years ago we had one of our best family holidays driving from Parador to Parador in northern Spain: it was during grape-picking time in October when the weather was hot – but comfortably hot. Our children have fond memories of being plied with bunches of fresh sun-warmed grapes by cheery pickers (wherever we went, the children were the subject of great affectionate interest). If you thought you knew Spain, as its advertising campaign used to say, think again.

In producing this book I am grateful to all the tour operators who generously took the time to provide information about their holidays. As always I am also indebted to Sheila Barrett who did most of the hard work (and to Dan and Jessica Barrett who have shared much of the travelling).

Frank Barrett, November 1994

INTRODUCTION

There is no country in the world which the British think they know better than Spain – yet in many ways we could hardly know it less well. Through almost four decades it has consistently been the most popular holiday destination with UK travellers, so how can we possibly be accused of ignorance?

Well, did you know, for example, that – next to Switzerland – Spain is the second most mountainous country in Europe? In the most spectacular of these mountains, the Picos de Europa in Spain's green north, you can still find bears and wolves roaming free.

Few British are aware that Arabs – the Moors – occupied Spain for over seven hundred years from 711 to 1492, leaving a rich cultural legacy – marvellous buildings like the Mezquita in Cordoba. Yet for most British people, knowledge of Spain's history probably extends no further back than General Franco and dimly held recollections of the Spanish Civil War.

Mention Spanish hotels and British travellers tend to summon up garish images of ugly Costa concrete tower blocks. Yet with its chain of Paradors – buildings of historic importance that have been converted into hotels, some of them among the best hotels in the world – Spain has one of the world's most excellent hotel chains.

The Spain, therefore, that most travellers have come to know (or that they think they know) is Package Holiday Spain, a semi-mythical place largely created by British tour operators and maintained by canny Spanish entrepreneurs.

Package Holiday Spain is the place that all smart travellers love to hate (even though its detractors have probably never visited it). They know that it is largely a world of donkeys in straw hats, crass flamenco folkloric shows, souvenir castanets, paella parties, wet T-shirt competitions, bars offering tea 'like Mother makes it' and pints of warm insipid English beer.

This is conceivably how it may have been in Benidorm or

1

Magaluf in the Sixties when these fast-growing resorts were almost wholly patronized by the British. But these days the main Spanish holiday places have to look to Central Europe and Scandinavia, as much as to the UK, for their livelihood – so they have gradually lost the worst aspects of British package holiday culture (besides, these excesses were always made out to be much worse than they really were).

Sure, on the Costas, you will still find your Queen Vic Bars and Rovers Return Pubs with their endless happy hours. But nowadays you are just as likely to find manifestations of the new cosmopolitan Euro culture: pasta and pizza joints, Benetton clothes shops, Swatch watch emporia and high-tech high-energy discos.

But it remains true to say that for the most part genuine Spanish life barely intrudes into the carefully contrived world of Package Holiday Spain. Of course this situation suits many of the people who visit it right down to the ground. For travellers who prefer a bottle of tomato ketchup to a dash of olive oil and who would rather quench their thirst with Red Barrel than Rioja, Package Holiday Spain must seem the perfect place.

But over the past few years, travellers and tour operators alike have woken up to the fact that there is much, much more to Spain than a thin strip of overdeveloped coastline that runs along the Mediterranean coast from Barcelona to Gibraltar. There is another Spain. To use an expression which has become something of a cliché, there is Real Spain. And there is a fast-growing market of travellers keen to enjoy its pleasures.

In this book I shall try to offer a guide to the holiday opportunities offered by both Spains (and the tour operators who feature them).

The Real Spain is tailor-made for independent travel, there is an increasing list of specialist operators who offer self-catering holidays to traditional Spanish houses in northern Spain, for example – and companies who will painstakingly plan fly-drive trips around the Paradors on your behalf.

But you would be wrong to reject Package Holiday Spain out of hand. For a family holiday, it offers great potential. One of its principal attractions, of course, is price. The profusion of charter flights and the huge supply of hotel rooms and apartment blocks provides the infrastructure for very low-cost packages, ideal for those in search of something cheap and cheerful.

It's interesting, however, to reflect that while we now associate Spain with holidays, its status as a holiday destination is a very recent phenomenon. Until the mid-Fifties those who travelled abroad on summer holiday went to France, Italy or the Swiss lakes. Spain was too hot, too undeveloped, too poor and too much under the control of Franco.

Spain's transformation over the past twenty years has been substantially helped by the influence of tourism. Visitors brought prosperity, they brought infrastructure, they helped change the political climate so that after Franco's death, the Spanish demanded the sort of democracy enjoyed by its annual horde of visitors.

In the political dictionary of -ism's, tourism can be shown to have been a force for change every bit as significant as Marxism.

THE RISE OF SPAIN

I first visited Spain some thirty years ago when, as a child, I travelled on a cruise ship that called at the island of Majorca. This was the dawn of Package Holiday Spain: Majorca, like the rest of the country, was still largely a place of dusty roads, scorched fields worked by hand and houses that displayed grinding poverty.

While the rest of Western Europe was entering in a new era of post-War prosperity, fascist Spain remained stuck in a feudal system that had changed little since the expulsion of the Moors. The rich man owned the big house and the land, the poor people worked for him.

Since Spain was politically – and economically – shunned by its neighbours there seemed little prospect for change or improvement. Until, with the advent of tourism the world changed. Many people you speak to in Spain today have vivid memories of that change.

There are those in the town of Calvia who can still clearly recall that summer's day in 1955 when a motor-coach filled with holidaying Britons and Swedes nosed its way down the dusty single-track road that led from Palma to Paguera. Unable to find a spare hotel room in the Majorcan capital, the travellers headed towards the west coast of the island – driving from town to town in search of bed and board. Calvia's inhabitants have good reason to remember – it was the day their lives changed.

Antonio Pallicer, the deputy mayor of Calvia Town Council and a member of the island's parliament, is the Councillor of Tourism. His dominion, said to be the richest municipal borough in the whole of Spain, includes the sprawling package holiday conurbations of Magaluf and Palma Nova. From the splendid new town hall high in Calvia, built on the new prosperity of tourism, Pallicer can gaze down towards the tower-blocked coastline – and marvel at the pace of change.

Pallicer was ten in that fateful summer of '55. Until then his life promised to be as hard as that suffered by preceding generations of his family.

The only work was on the land; the only employers were a few improvident landowners. Pallicer's parents had received no formal education. Following the normal practice, they started work at the age of eight, looking after the olive, almond and carob trees or tending the sheep, goats and cows.

The only prospect of prosperity was to leave Majorca and work abroad. Pallicer's grandfather spent three hard years in Cuba making charcoal and harvesting sponges. He made enough money eventually to return to Majorca, others who left the island were not so fortunate.

Antonio Pallicer is at pains to point out that the people of Calvia seldom yearn for the past – there were no good old days. 'Everybody tried to be happy. But there was always hunger, there was no education, no culture, no prospects. Life was very hard.'

Like the Caribbean natives who first sighted Columbus's ships, the citizens of Calvia who encountered those pioneer expeditionary tourists in 1955 could not have guessed that these strange aliens were the unlikely vanguard of a massive invasion.

Within a year tour operators were arriving in Calvia, eager to encourage the building of new hotels. On the marshy lowlands of Magaluf, where no-one had thought to live among the foul malarial swamps, holiday companies desired to build a resort. Prospective hotel developers were offered a no-lose deal. Build a hotel, they were told, and you will recover your costs in two years – from the third year there will be pure profit.

On an island where even the landowners were as poor as church mice, the prospect of riches inspired a sort of gold fever. The Franco regime in Madrid, desperate for foreign currency, was happy to sanction all the hotel construction that was wanted.

By the age of thirteen, Pallicer had found a job as a hotel bellboy. When he was fifteen he had saved enough money to come to London in 1960 to learn English at a school in Bayswater. 'For the first time I saw television. For the first time I saw democracy. I met Germans and French who were architects and engineers: they had an education – I wanted an education.'

With his knowledge of English, Pallicer quickly worked his way up through the hotel trade – from bellboy to concierge and into management, saving his pay so that eventually he could put himself through university. 'Tourism changed my life,' says Pallicer: 'Tourism changed all our lives.'

While the lives of the Spanish have certainly changed, the most noticeable impact of tourism has been on the landscape. Several years ago I remember visiting a fish restaurant on La Carihuela in Torremolinos. The Carihuela used to be the base for the town's fishermen but now it has been absorbed into the all-embracing tourist business. On the wall of the fish restaurant was an enlarged photograph of a beach which showed a few down-at-heel buildings alongside some fishing boats.

'Torremolinos 1952' said the caption. Most people who looked at the photograph and then read the caption responded with a swift double-take. Torremolinos? Impossible.

Yet until the Fifties, beyond the occasional coach party from Gibraltar, Torremolinos was untouched by tourism and tourists. It really was a small impoverished Andalucian fishing village. The invention of the package holiday in the Fifties and the development of the low-cost package deal in the Sixties changed things with astonishing speed.

It is now a forest of tower-block hotels, a glitzy strip of bars, fast-food places and neon-lit night clubs. Garish? Certainly. But at night it exudes a noisy, bustling ambience unique to Spain. For those who enjoy it, no other resort will do.

But this is only one small part of Spain: like all the other heavily developed resort towns, it occupies just a tiny fraction of Spain.

Head out of Malaga airport and turn left up the coast, or inland towards Granada and you can leave the overdeveloped resorts far behind. Within an hour you can be in some peaceful sun-baked white village, sipping a glass of dry sherry and nibbling olives in the shaded part of a village square. No discos, no hamburgers, no crass souvenir shops: few people will speak English but most will be keen to offer the simple polite formalities of traditional Spanish hospitality.

From the brochures of the big operators, Spain may seem like one sun-and-sand beach destination, with a couple of 'historic' daytrips for those keen for a break from the beach. In reality, the country is a complex multi-faceted place, offering more holiday potential than even France or Italy – with the advantage that, away from the coast and a few big cities, tourism has barely established itself.

Whatever side of the country you prefer, there can be no doubt that Spain dominates the British package holiday market. In Summer 1994, Spain filled five of the top ten selling destinations. (In first place was Majorca, second Tenerife, fourth Ibiza, seventh Minorca and ninth Gran Canaria). Of all package holidays sold, 45 per cent were to Spanish destinations.

Spain's success in 1994 can be partly explained by a more favourable exchange rate with the peseta. The truth, however, is that Spain is always the favourite: no other destination can match in terms of bed spaces offered and the competitive cost of flying there. Spain will always be number one.

As the country now tries to shake off its image as a place that can only offer cheap sun-and-sand packages, it hopes to extend the horizon of tourism, and could lift its share of the UK market yet higher.

Spain will always surprise us. Dip into this guide and I can guarantee some formidable holiday surprises.

THE BEST OF SPAIN

In this book I hope to alert you to the best of the holiday possibilities offered by Spain. To provide a taste of the best the country has to offer, here is my selection of Spanish superlatives – I would be pleased to hear your nominations (the best recommendations will earn a free edition of the revised *Family Spain*).

Best Spanish Tour Operator

If any operator can be said to offer the best of 'Real Spain' then it must be Mundi Color, which has long been the leading

Spanish specialist offering what it describes as 'holidays for discerning travellers'. Its 'Discover Spain' programme features everything from packages to the national parks of Spain and gastronomy and wine tours to holidays on the lesser known Canary Islands such as La Gomera and El Hierro. See page 117.

Best Hotel Chain

Spain's Paradors are arguably not just the best hotel chain in Spain but perhaps one of the finest in the world. A government-owned selection of properties that are either buildings of historic importance or else in outstandingly beautiful locations, each Parador has something special to offer.

They are no longer cheap, the service is about what you would expect from a state-run establishment, facilities are often basic, restaurants tend to offer an uninspiring selection of food, the staff are short on customer contact skills – but despite all this, the Paradors are a genuine treat. See page 50.

Best Spanish City Break

Twenty years ago, people knew little about Barcelona beyond the fact that it had a football team of some note, it boasted some extraordinary architecture by Gaudi and it had played a leading part in the Spanish Civil War (these events were memorably recorded by George Orwell in his marvellous book *Homage to Catalonia*).

Through the Eighties, Barcelona rapidly earned a reputation among 'those who know' as one of the liveliest cities in Europe.

From the dark years of Franco, Barcelona sprang forth as a vibrant, innovative, go-getting place. It was fitting that it won the right to stage the 1992 Olympic Games, an event that once and for all drew the world's attention to Barcelona's stunning achievements.

As a weekend break place, it is almost perfect. A fascinating historic heart: the Ramblas is marvellous for aimless wandering; good museums aplenty – the Picasso museum has one of Europe's finest collections; and an unrivalled public transport system to get you around. See page 121.

Best Spanish Holiday Region

Imagine Cornwall with lots of sunshine, good food, excellent wine and a local population that has a deep-seated love for fiestas and public festivities. This provides some small idea of Galicia's attraction.

Located on Spain's north-west coast, Galicia is as far removed as can be imagined from most people's idea of the Spanish Costas. First, there is no baking heat; second, the coastline is decidedly Celtic; third, there are hardly any tourists. Go now, and beat the rush. See page 88.

Best Spanish Treat

If you've been to a *tapas* bar in Britain, I'm afraid it will provide you with no indication of what a genuine Spanish *tapas* bar is like. Here it's a yuppie night out, in Spain *tapas* are a traditional bar snack enjoyed by everybody. 'Snack' is a bit of a misnomer: the selection of *tapas* on offer in most bars provides the basis for a pretty substantial meal: cheese, seafood, Spanish omelette, spicy red sausage, cooked meats. You pick and mix and pay according to the size of portion you get. Given that the Spanish eat late, a selection of *tapas* provides a very acceptable alternative to dinner. (For vegetarians like me, *tapas* are an even better alternative to dinner!)

THE WORST OF SPAIN

- Bullfighting. Ernest Hemingway could try and rationalize it all he liked (the nobility of the animal tested against the bravery of the man etc) but when it gets down to it, bullfighting is a pretty nasty business. Despite what the campaigners say, it doesn't just exist for tourists: Spaniards tend to be enthusiastic bullfight supporters (live fights are regularly shown on the television). As well as the normal bull-fights, many small towns stage their own Pamplona-esque bull runnings: a makeshift arena is set up in a town square and the local youths taunt a succession of bullocks (with sometimes serious consequence for the local youths). Cruelty to animals is something that appears not to bother many Spaniards.

- Mealtimes. Spaniards eat terrifyingly late (see *tapas* above). Many Spanish restaurants (that cater largely for the locals) will not start serving breakfast before 8am, lunch begins at 1pm and will continue until 4pm. As a result dinner does not commence until 9pm. If you like eating early, try the *tapas* or invest in a few bags of crisps!

- Over-development. Spain has suffered badly from being the very first mass-market package holiday destination. Developers bent over backwards to accommodate the demands of British tour operators who subscribed to the basic marketing principle of piling it high and selling it cheap. Oranges may look all right piled high – hotel rooms don't. Some Spanish regions have learnt from their mistakes – other areas seem to want to go on piling it high...

- Spain snobs. A new breed of Spanish traveller has emerged: the Spanish big head. The person who claims to be the complete expert on all things Spanish. Fluent in Catalan, he will tell you all the best fish restaurants on a street in Barcelona; he will reveal how he was offered the chance to train as a bull-fighter; he will play you his complete collection of Gypsy King records etc. Tell him you think Magaluf is a much under-rated place...

I hope you enjoy *Family Spain*: if you have any comments, suggestions or recommendations, please write to me at PO Box 67, Bath.

If you are travelling to Spain for a holiday, may I wish you a very happy and very successful trip!

1

PLANNING A HOLIDAY

There are a number of key decisions you need to take before
getting to the point of making a firm booking and handing
over your money. Do you want to buy an organized package
from an operator or would you rather arrange your own
package?

The advantage of buying an organized package is conve-
nience. The tour operator does all the work for you. The disad-
vantage is that the holiday may not be exactly what you want.
There is unlikely to be any great difference in price between
buying from an operator and doing it yourself. The operator
makes a profit out of your holiday arrangements, of course, but
usually as a bulk buyer of travel it benefits from economies of
scale, a benefit which is passed on to a greater or lesser extent
to the customer.

The main motivation for organizing your own package
would be because you are keen to do something on your
holiday that falls outside the range of packages on the market.
You would like to go cycling in Old Castile, for example, or
walking in Extremadura.

In this guide we have listed the main operators and their
sun-and-sand packages – and also the main specialist companies and their huge range of activity holidays. Here you should
find something to fit your particular requirements.

The next main decision you have to make is: which Spain are
you planning to visit? Package Holiday Spain or, for want of a
better description, Real Spain? Package Holiday Spain offers
lookalike Mediterranean resorts where you are never more
than a few minutes from a pizza parlour or a chip shop, and
where the newsagent will have today's copy of the *Daily Mail*.

Real Spain is quite a different proposition. Life is uncompro-
misingly Spanish: the shopkeeper will not speak English
(though his son or daughter certainly will!), meals will be late
and the food will be unmistakably local. But there will be the

excitement of being in a foreign country, and you will have the chance to visit astonishing places and see remarkable sights – all as a result of your own clever endeavours. In this guide we attempt to guide you to the best of Real Spain.

The secret of any successful holiday is research, research and more research. People tend to have a bad holiday because they booked the wrong holiday: they went with the wrong operator or they chose the wrong destination (sometimes both). Before choosing read this book, read other relevant books, talk to people who have visited the bits of Spain you may be interested in. Talk over with your family what you would all like to do: is the priority, for example, sightseeing or sunbathing? When you have all the relevant information, phone around the likely operators, compare prices – and then make your booking. You will probably only have one big holiday this year – make it count!

FINDING OUT INFORMATION

The Spanish tourist office is located at 57–58 St James's St, London SW1A 1LD (071-499 0901). There is theoretically a telephone information service available from 9am to 4.30pm Monday to Friday: in practice, the line is almost constantly engaged. The most effective way of gathering information is to visit the office in person (there is an excellent range of leaflets on display). The tourist office promises to answer every letter it receives: to expedite a reply enclose a good-sized self-addressed stamped envelope.

Guidebooks

More guidebooks have been written about Spain than about almost any other country in the world, probably exceeding even the number that cover France. They are everything from straightforward destination guides to a wide range of books on activities like cycling and specialist pursuits such as botany and birdwatching. Just as interesting to read is the fascinating selection of travel literature available on Spain. These are some of the better books to look out for:

Spain: The Rough Guide (Penguin, £9.99) by Mark Ellingham and John Fisher: marvellously comprehensive guide for the independent traveller, packed with useful advice and information.

Cadogan Southern Spain: Andalucia and Gibraltar (Cadogan, £9.99) by Dana Facaros and Michael Pauls: well written, informative guide.

Landscapes of Cataluna: Delta del Ebro and Puertos de Beceite (Sunflower, £5.99) by Paul Jenner and Christine Smith: sound countryside guide for walkers and nature lovers.

Blue Guide Barcelona (A&C Black, £8.99) by Michael Jacobs: reliable account of the city's history and main sights.

The Way of St James: The Pilgrimage Route to Santiago de Compostela (Lascelles, £7.95) by Dr Elias Valina Sampedro.

Karen Brown's Spanish Country Inns and Itineraries (Karen Brown, £8.99): useful guide for finding interesting accommodation off the beaten track.

Travel Literature

South From Granada (Penguin, £6.99) by Gerald Brenan: a classic of travel literature – an account of the writer's life in the Alpujarras in the 1920s.

As I Walked Out One Midsummer Morning (Penguin, £5.99) by Laurie Lee: the wonderfully evocative account of a journey on foot across Spain before the outbreak of the Spanish Civil War.

Tales of the Alhambra (Darf, £30) by Washington Irving: fascinating tales of Granada's Moorish palace.

Winter in Majorca (Academy Press, £3) by George Sand: a must-read book for all visitors to Majorca, it tells of Sand's ill-fated winter spent in the monastery of Valldemossa with Chopin. The book is widely available in Majorca, particularly in Valldemossa.

Specialist Travel Bookshops in the UK include:

Daunt Books for Travellers, 83 Marylebone High Street, London W1 (071-224 2295): Fascinating shop owned and managed by James Daunt where books are arranged geographically.

Stanfords, 12–14 Long Acre, London WC2E 9LP (071-836 1321): Stanfords has been serving the needs of the independent traveller since 1851; the management claims that Stanfords' sixteen-strong staff is ready to offer expert advice on the shop's stock of 20,000 maps and books. Stanfords' can also handle inquiries by phone or mail.

Travel Bookshop, 13 Blenheim Crescent, London W11 2EE (071-229 5260): New and second-hand books with over 12,000 titles covering guidebooks as well as background works on art, history and wildlife – and also fiction. Mail order service: send s.a.e. for special lists. Credit card orders taken on telephone.

Travellers' Bookshop, 25 Cecil Court, London WC2N 4EZ (071-836 9132): The shop has a good selection of new and second-hand travel books.

Waterstones, 121–125 Charing Cross Road, London WC2 (071-434 4291): The Charing Cross branch has the best range of travel books, but the other thirteen shops in London and the eighty-seven elsewhere in the UK have a comprehensive range.

PASSPORTS

To enter Spain you do not need the full British passport: the twelve-month Visitors' passport (BVP) available from Post Offices is sufficient. However, this may change: the Spanish government has said that it no longer wishes to accept the BVP and, since the British government is already keen to scrap the BVP, its future seems in doubt.

If you take regular holidays abroad, the full ten-year passport available from the Passport Offices listed below is the best value. An application form is available from main post offices. A thirty-two-page passport costs £15; a forty-eight-page passport costs £22.50.

Passport Offices

Liverpool
Passport Office,
5th Floor,
India Buildings,
Water Street,
Liverpool L2 0QZ
051-237 3010

London
Passport Office,
Clive House,
70 Petty France,
London SW1H 9HD
071-279 3434

Newport
Passport Office,
Olympia House,
Upper Dock Street,
Newport,
Gwent NPT 1XA
0633 244500/244292

Scotland
Passport Office,
3 Northgate,
96 Milton Street,
Cowcaddens,
Glasgow G4 0BT
041-332 0271

Peterborough
Passport Office,
Aragon Court,
Northminster Road,
Peterborough PE1 1QG
0733 895555

Northern Ireland
Passport Office,
Hampton House,
47-53 High Street,
Belfast BT1 2QS
0232 232371

DRIVING LICENCE

You will need to show your UK driving licence before you can hire a car (so will other members of the party if they wish to share the driving). An International Driver's Permit is not necessary.

HEALTH AND INSURANCE

There is no need for any vaccinations or other medical precautions. The only precaution necessary is a financial one. You need to have insurance which will not only be sufficient to cover you against medical costs but will also offer cover against other routine hazards such as cancellation and theft. If you wish to take advantage of the reciprocal health agreement that allows free medical treatment in Spain, you will need to have form E111, available from main post offices (but even with the E111, health insurance is still advisable).

If you are driving to Spain in your own car, you will need to arrange a Green Card which provides you with the insurance cover on the Continent that you have in the UK (without the Green Card, your cover will be reduced to Third Party only). Also consider taking out one of the motoring rescue policies such as AA Five Star which will offer assistance if you have an accident or suffer a mechanical breakdown.

Taking money

For any travel overseas nowadays a credit card is an almost indispensable companion. When we travel as a family, a credit card is our principal means of payment. If you dislike the concept of credit cards (this is understandable!), travellers' cheques and Eurocheques will do just as well – but they are a less efficient and more expensive means of paying bills abroad.

We always take a couple of hundred pounds in the local currency as a start as well as a couple of hundred pounds in Sterling as a back-up. Many bills such as hotel bills, car-hire charges, petrol etc can be paid directly by credit card. If you need further amounts of local currency these can be obtained with your credit card from most cash dispensers in Spain. Since these machines occasionally swallow cards for no obvious reason, it may be wise not to travel with one credit card as your sole source of funds.

If you take travellers' cheques keep a separate note of their numbers and a note of which ones you have cashed (you will need this if they are stolen). Also keep a photocopy of the vital details of your passport and keep this in a safe place (if your passport is lost or stolen, this photocopy may be sufficient to get you home without the hassle of getting a new passport issued by the local consular office).

2

GETTING TO SPAIN

Spain and charter flights are practically synonymous. The vast majority of the British who travel to Spain do so on a charter flight. Charter flights have the advantage of being both relatively inexpensive and very convenient. Charter flights to the principal Spanish holiday airports, Palma and Malaga, are available from nearly every UK regional airport. The main UK airports offer charter flights to all the major Spanish holiday airports.

The charter flight now so thoroughly dominates the market that scheduled airlines have been forced to concentrate their efforts on the main business travel routes, mainly to Barcelona and Madrid.

In the past five years, an increasing number of travellers have been taking their own car to Spain. Brittany Ferries which has steadily developed the market with its service from Plymouth to Santander in northern Spain was worried that it would lose out in 1993 when P&O European Ferries launched a rival route from Portsmouth to Bilbao. It need not have worried. The new route didn't halve Brittany's business – it helped to grow the market, apparently doubling the number of people travelling by ferry to Spain.

As you can see from the fare table below, taking the car by ferry to Spain is not a cheap option. The ferry companies know that they can charge a premium rate for relieving people of the tedium and inconvenience of driving through France (which will certainly involve the added expense of staying at least one night en route).

But as the recommended routes below show, driving through France is not such a difficult business. All but a mile of the drive from Calais to Barcelona is on motorway – although you would not be advised to attempt the thirteen-hour drive in one day. (You may also find the £27 motorway tolls something of a disincentive!)

For a family, the attraction of taking your own car is that you can throw everything you will need in the back, meaning that you can take many of the comforts of home to your holiday destination (an important consideration when children are involved).

Flying and hiring a car might work out a cheaper option but the standard of hire cars, particularly from local independent specialists, has never filled me with great confidence (even the major companies sometimes produce cars in a sorry state of repair).

FLYING TO SPAIN

Direct Scheduled Flights from the UK

(Iberia, the Spanish airline, can also offer connecting flights to other airports including San Sebastian, Pamplona, Santander, Oviedo, Santiago, La Coruna, Vitoria, Vigo, Seville, Granada, Jerez, Almeria, Ibiza, Mahon, Tenerife, Las Palmas and Lanzarote.)

From	To	Airline
Birmingham	Barcelona	British Airways
Birmingham	Malaga	British Airways
London Gatwick	Madrid	British Airways
London Gatwick	Madrid	Viva
London Gatwick	Malaga	British Airways
London Gatwick	Malaga	Viva
London Heathrow	Alicante	Viva
London Heathrow	Barcelona	British Airways
London Heathrow	Barcelona	Iberia
London Heathrow	Bilbao	British Airways
London Heathrow	Bilbao	Iberia
London Heathrow	Madrid	British Airways
London Heathrow	Madrid	British Airways
London Heathrow	Malaga	Viva
London Heathrow	Palma	British Midland
London Heathrow	Palma	Viva
London Heathrow	Santiago	Iberia
London Heathrow	Valencia	Iberia
London Stansted	Oviedo	Aviaco

From	To	Airline
London Stansted	Zaragoza	Iberia
Manchester	Barcelona	British Airways
Manchester	Barcelona	Iberia
Manchester	Madrid	British Airways
Manchester	Malaga	British Airways

Airline Telephone Numbers

British Airways 0345 222111
Iberia/Aviaco/Viva 071-830 0011

CHANNEL TUNNEL

Folkestone to Calais on Le Shuttle costs £260 (0303 271100)

FERRIES

How peak July/August 1994 fares and services compare

Route	Operator	Daily sailings	Journey time	Return fare* (4.5m car & 2 adults)
Direct Services to Spain				
Portsmouth–Bilbao	P&O Ferries	2 per week	33hrs	£680
Plymouth–Santander	Brittany Ferries	2 per week	24hrs	£544
Other Routes to the Continent				
Hull–Rotterdam	North Sea Ferries	1	14hrs	£358
Hull–Zeebrugge	North Sea Ferries	1	14hrs	£358
Felixstowe–Zeebrugge	P&O Ferries	2	5hrs 45 mins 8hrs (night)	£275-£300

Route	Operator	Daily sailings	Journey time	Return fare*
Harwich– Hook of Holland	Stena	2	6hrs 30 mins 8hrs 30 mins (night)	£200– £323*
Ramsgate–Dunkerque	Sally	5	2hrs 30 mins	£190– £255
Ramsgate–Oostende	Sally	6	4hrs	£190– £255
Dover–Calais	Hover– Speed	14 h'cft	35 mins	£213– £318
Dover–Calais	Stena	25	1hr 30 mins	£200– £300
Dover–Calais	P&O Ferries	25	1hr 15 mins	£128– £300
Folkestone–Boulogne	Hover- speed Seacat	5/6	55 mins	£200– £290
Newhaven–Dieppe	Stena	4	4hrs	£216– £296
Portsmouth–Le Havre	P&O Ferries	3	5hrs 45 mins 7–9hrs (night)	£212– £317
Portsmouth–Caen	Brittany Ferries	3	6hrs	£201– £316
Portsmouth– Cherbourg	P&O Ferries	3	4hrs 45 mins 8hrs 45 mins– 9hrs 45 mins (night)	£164– £292
Portsmouth–St Malo	Brittany Ferries	1	9hrs	£298– £338
Southampton– Cherbourg	Stena	1/2	6hrs day 8hrs night	£204– £342
Poole–Cherbourg	Truckline Ferries	1/2	4hrs 15 mins	£225– £296
Poole–St Malo	Brittany Ferries	4 per week	8hrs 9hrs 30 mins (night)	£298– £338

Route	Operator	Daily sailings	Journey time	Return fare*
Plymouth–Roscoff	Brittany	1–3	6hrs	£254–£324

Exact fare depends upon the time of travel: on longer crossings, particularly for night sailings, you may have the additional cost of on board cabin accommodation. Cheaper fares are available for short-break crossings.

The Operators

Brittany Ferries 0705 827701
Hoverspeed 0304 240241
North Sea Ferries 0482 77177
P&O European Ferries 0304 203388
Sealink Stena Line 0233 647047
Sally Line 0843 595522
Truckline 0705 827701

DRIVING TO SPAIN

Below we list some of the main routes for driving down through France to Spain. Have your car serviced shortly in advance of your departure. The main cause of breakdowns on the Continent is a problem with the cooling system of the engine: make sure that the radiator and all hoses are carefully checked – get worn ones replaced. Get the necessary kit for converting your headlights so that you don't blind oncoming drivers when you switch from main beam. As a further precaution, it may be worth taking out one of the accident and breakdown insurance policies offered by companies like the AA, RAC and Europ Assistance: expect to pay around £50 for fourteen days' cover.

The main cause of accidents when driving long distance is tiredness. Take frequent breaks: stop every hour on the service areas for a walk to stay fresh. If you feel as if you are going to fall asleep, stop and go to sleep: if it's already dark, find somewhere to stay the night. (Off the French motorway there are plenty of new motel chains offering rooms from as little as £16 per night.)

• As an alternative to driving through France, you could use Motorail and put your car on the train. French Railways (071-409 3518) offers services from Calais to Biarritz, Toulouse and Narbonne all of which are handily placed for access to Spain. The return fare for Calais to Biarritz, for example, is £365 for a car and driver travelling second class: an additional adult costs £84 and children aged four to eleven cost £42 each: on board accommodation costs from £10 per berth in a six-berth compartment.

Recommended Routes

Michelin recommended route for travelling from Calais to Barcelona

Total distance 864 miles (1383kms), expected driving time 13 hours 25minutes (863 miles/1381kms [13hrs 6mins] are on motorway: motorway tolls will cost around £27).

Numbers of Michelin maps which cover the route: 989, 990, 51 and 443.

Time		*kms*
1 00:00	Calais (2km)	0000
	Take the A16 towards Dunkerque, Bethune	
	Continue on the A16 for 3km	
	Take the A26 towards Reims, Paris, Arras	
	Continue on the A26 for 107km	
2 01:06	(Arras)	0112
	Take the A1 towards Arras-Est, Paris	
	Continue on the A1 for 159.5km	
	Take the A3 towards Paris–Est, Bobigny	
	Continue on the A3 for 10km	
	Join the A86 following the signs for A4, Metz, Nancy	
	Continue on the A86 for 7km	
	Take the A4 in the direction of Paris, Creteil	
	Continue on the A4 for 3km	
	Join the A86 in the direction of Creteil, Troyes	
	Continue on the A86 for 13.5km	
	Join the A6 towards Bordeaux, Nantes	
	Continue on the A6 for 447.5km	
3 07:20	(Lyon)	0752
	Join the A7 for 95.5km	

4 08:14 (Valence)   0848
          Continue on the A7 for 101km

5 09:10 (Orange)   0949
          A9 towards Nimes, Montpellier
          Continue on the A9 for 14km

6 09:18 (Avignon)   0963
          Continue on the A9 for 33km

7 09:36 (Nimes)   0996
          Continue on the A9 for 43.5km

8 10:00 (Montpellier)   1039
          Continue on the A9 for 163.5km

9 11:30 (Perpignan)   1203
          Continue on the A9 for 24km

10   Spanish frontier
          Continue on the A7 for 138.5km
          Follow the signs for Barcelona Este
          Take the A17 for 7.5km
          Follow the sign for Barcelona
          Take the A18 for 2km
          Take 'II Cinturo' for 0.5km
          Continue on the B10 for 4km
          After 3.5km arrive in:

11 13:12 Barcelona   1383

Michelin recommended route for travelling from Bilbao to Seville
Total distance 577 miles (924kms), expected driving time 9 hours 5minutes (571 miles/915kms [8hrs 54mins] are on motorway: motorway tolls will cost around £10).
  The Michelin maps which cover this route are: 442, 444 and 446.

Time   *kms*

1 00:00 Bilbao (2km)   0000
          Follows the signs for Miranda de Ebro, Gasteiz

23

Take the A8 for 3.5km
Follow the sign for Miranda de Ebro
Continue on the A68 for 69.5km

2 00:42 (Miranda de Ebro)   0075
Follow the sign for Burgos
Take the A1 for 85.5km

3 01:29 (Burgos)   0161
Follow the sign for Madrid
Take the NI for 39.5km
Follow the sign for Madrid
Continue on the NI for 184km
Take the M30 for 12km
Take the NIV for 1km
Follow the signs for Valdemoro, Aranjuez

4 03:48 Madrid (1.5km)   0397
Continue on the NIV for 378.5km

5 07:35 (Cordoba)   0777
NIV for 137.5km

6 08:55 Seville (4.5km)   0915
Take the Isla de la Cartuja exit

7 09:05 Seville (5km)   0924

Michelin Recommended Route for Travelling from Le Havre to Santiago de Compostela
Total distance 1064 miles (1703kms), expected driving time 18 hours 22minutes (695 miles/1113kms [10 hrs 21mins] are on motorway: motorway tolls will cost around £25). The Michelin maps which cover this route are: 989, 990, 55 and 441.

Time   *kms*

1   00:00 Le Havre (1km)   0000
Take the N15 for 7km
Join the A15 towards A13, Paris, Rouen
Take the A131 for 18km
Continue on the N182 for 2km

2   00:28   Pont de Tancarville (2km)   0028
            Take the A131 for 15km

3   00:39   (Pont-Audemer)   0045
            Take the A13 towards Paris, Rouen
            Continue on the A13 for 28km

4   00:54   (Rouen)   0073
            Continue on the A13 for 111km

5   01:55   (Rocquencourt)   0184
            Take the A12 towards St-Quentin-en-Yonne
            Continue on the A12 for 6.5km

6   01:58   (Bois-d'Arcy)   0191
            Take the N12 in the direction of Versailles-Satory
            Continue on the N12 for 3km

7   02:00   (Saint-Cyr-l'Ecole)   0194
            Take the N286 for 5.5km

8   02:03   (Versailles)   0199
            Take the A86 for 5km
            Take the N118 towards Orleans
            Continue on the N118 for 16.5km

9   02:20   (Les Ulis)   0221
            Take the A10 towards Chartres, Orleans
            Continue on the A10 for 200.5km

10 04:10   (Tours)   0421
            A10 for 100.5km

11 05:08   (Poitiers)   0522
            Continue on the A10 for 243km

12 07:21   (Carbon-Blanc)   0765
            Leave the A10 at 'Sortie 1', Arcachon, Bayonne
            Take the N230 for 10km

13 07:27   (Bordeaux)   0775
            Take the A630 for 10km

14 07:32 (Pessac)   0785
            At 'Sortie 15', take the A63 towards Arcachon
            Continue on the A63 for 46km

15 07:58 (Belin-Boliet)   0831
            Take the N10 towards Hendaye
            Continue on the N10 for 92.5km

16 08:59 (Saint-Geours-de-Maremne)   0923
            Take the A63 towards Hendaye
            Continue on the A63 for 44.5km

17 09:23 (Biarritz)   0968
            Continue on the A63 for 22km

18 Spanish frontier
            Take the A8 for 124.5km
            Leave the motorway at the 'Bilbao Oeste' exit

19 10:45 (Bilbao)   1114
            Take the N634 for 7km
            After 4.5km take the A8 for 14.5km

20 11:01 (Castro-Urdiales)   1140
            Take the Castro-Urdiales exit
            Continue on the N634 for 19.5km

21 11:23 Laredo (0.5km)   1160
            At Colindres join the A8 for 7.5km
            Take the Santona exit and join the N634
            for 19.5km

22 11:48 Hoznayo (1.5km)   1187
            Proceed on the A8 for 14.5km

23 11:58 (Santander)   1203
            Continue on the A8 for 4.5km following the
            signs forArce, Torrelavega
            Join the A67 for 15.5km
            At Torrelavega join the N634 for 153km
            After 14.5km follow the signs for Gijon, Avilos
            Join the A66 for 13km

At Aviles take the A8 for 12km
Continue on the N632 for 55.5km

| 24 | 15:18 | Canero | 1471 |
| | | Continue on the N634 for 94.5km | |

| 25 | 16:33 | (Mondonedo) | 1566 |
| | | After 4km join the N634 for 47km | |

26	17:13	Baamonde	1617
		Continue on the NVI for 18.5km	
		Join the N634 for 64.5km	

| 27 | 18:22 | Santiago de Compostela (3.5km) | 1703 |

Michelin recommended route for travelling from Santander to Seville
Total distance 573 miles (918kms), expected driving time
9 hours 42minutes (474 miles/759kms [7hrs 28mins] are on
motorway: motorway tolls will cost around £25). The Michelin
maps which cover this route are: 442, 444 and 446

	Time		*kms*
1	00:00	Santander (3km)	0000
		Join the N623 for 145.5km	
2	02:00	Burgos (1km)	0149
		Continue on the NI for 44km	
		Take the road to Madrid	
		Join the NI for 184km	
		Continue on the M30 for 12km	
		Join the NIV for 1km	
		Follow the sign for Valdemoro, Aranjuez	
3	04:24	Madrid (1.5km)	0391
		Continue on the NIV for 378.5km	
4	08:11	(Cordoba)	0771
		Continue on the NIV for 137.5km	
5	09:31	Seville (4.5km)	0908
		Take the Isla de la Cartuja exit	

6   09:42 Seville (5km)   0918

Michelin recommended route for travelling from Barcelona to Cadiz
Total distance 708 miles (1134kms), expected driving time 11
hours 48minutes (538 miles/862kms [8hrs 14mins] are on
motorway: motorway tolls will cost around £18).
The Michelin maps which cover this route are: 443, 444
and 446

Time		*kms*
1	00:00 Barcelona (6km) Take the A2 for 14km Follow the signs for Tarragona Take the A7 for 348.5km Leave the motorway at exit 328 for Madrid and Valencia	0000
2	03:35 (Valencia) Take the NIII for 131km Continue on the N320 for 15.5km Join the CU821 for 0.5km	0369
3	05:12 Villanueva de la Jara Take the N310 for 141km	0516
4	06:53 Manzanares (2km) Follow the signs for Valdepenas, Cordoba Take the NIV for 213km	0657
5	09:07 (Cordoba) Take the NIV for 146.5km Take the Sevilla Centro exit	0872
6	10:32 Sevilla Take the NIV for 11km	1018
7	10:40 (Dos Hermanas) Follow the signs for Cadiz Take the A4 for 41.5km Continue on the E5 for 50.5km Take exit 6 for Cadiz	1029

Join the N443 for 8.5km
Take the NIV for 4.5km

8   11:48 Cadiz   1134

3

Getting around in Spain

Internal Transport

Trains:

RENFE, the Spanish rail company, runs a comprehensive network of domestic rail services at prices much cheaper than for equivalent rail journeys in the UK. To coincide with the opening of Expo 92 in Seville, a new high-speed rail link was inaugurated from Madrid to Seville travelling via Cordoba. Domestic rail passes are very good value: a RENFE Tarjeta Turistica, offering three days' second class travel in any thirty-day period costs from around £75. Further information from British Rail stations.

Car Hire:

Spain is one of the cheapest countries in Europe for car hire. Expect to pay from around £105 per week during high season for the smallest car including unlimited mileage and all extras. Prices are low because competition is fierce: the low prices often translate into cars of poor quality. Before accepting a car, particularly from a small local independent company, check it thoroughly. Make sure, for example, that all the lights work; pay special attention to the tyres. Look to see that they are not worn or otherwise in poor condition. Look in the boot to see that there is both a jack (and a handle to operate the jack!) and a spare tyre (look also to see that this is in good condition). It is also worth asking how to use the jack: I have wasted more hours than I would care to remember fiddling around with jacks that I couldn't get to work properly.

    Car hire companies: Avis (081-848 8733); Budget (0800 181 181); Europcar (081-950 5050); Hertz (081-679 1799/0345 555 888).

ELECTRICITY

In Spain they have different plugs (the two-pin European style) but the same sort of 240V electricity.

USING THE PHONES

Little more than twenty years ago, public telephones were a great rarity in Spain. Now there seem to be more payphones around than there are in the UK (even the smallest, most remote mountain village will have a payphone that allows international direct-dial calls to the UK).

The phones take 5, 25 or 100 peseta pieces; card phones take cards to the value of 1000 and 2000 pesetas (the cards can be bought at tobacconists). If you are baffled by the instructions on the pay phones, go to a Telefonica office where you can call first and pay later.

To phone Britain from Spain, dial 07: wait for the international tone and then dial the UK code 44 followed by the local code minus the first 0.

If you are planning to phone home frequently, it's worth investing in a BT Charge Card or a Mercury Calling Card which allow you to charge the cost of the call to your own home phone bill.

SAFE TRAVELLING

Over the past few years, careful policing seems to have reduced the amount of street crime but it continues to be a problem in the major resorts.

It is mostly non-violent: of the bag-snatching and pickpocketing variety – opportunistic crime by people on the search for cash to sustain their drug habit. One of the main hazards to look out for, particularly in and around Madrid, Barcelona, Seville and along the Costa del Sol, are smash-and-grab raiders who travel on motorbikes and scooters cruising traffic jams on the look-out for valuables. They simply smash car windows, pull out cameras or handbags and drive quickly away. Another hazard are the roadside thieves who pose as 'good samaritans' to people suffering from car and tyre problems. The thieves typically attempt to divert the driver's attention by pointing out a mechanical problem and then steal items from the vehicle while the driver is looking elsewhere. The problem is said to be particularly acute with vehicles rented at Madrid's Barajas airport.

Beware of someone in an overtaking car apparently telling you that you have a flat tyre and should pull over. This is frequently the prelude to a smash-and-grab raid.

It is wise to be careful with valuables like handbags and cameras: keep them across your body in front of you where you can hold them with a protective hand. If you are staying in a hotel, lock your passports, tickets and other non-essential valuables in the hotel safe. Check with the hotel or local tourist office on the areas best avoided day or night.

If you leave items of value in the car, make sure they are locked away in the boot or kept out of sight under a seat. People never leave car radios in their cars in Spain: they nearly all have the sort that you can take out of the car (you frequently see people in cafes and bars with their radio safely on the table in front of them!).

If someone does make a grab for your handbag, do not attempt to fight back. It is better to lose your handbag than your life.

4

SELF-CATERING (AND SWAPPING)

For most people who take a self-catering holiday in Spain, it is a simple matter of picking out an apartment from the self-catering programme of one of the major operators. These apartments tend to be tower blocks indistinguishable from the tower-block hotels (in fact in many Spanish resorts, tower-block hotels are being converted for use as apartments: as a business self-catering is more profitable as it requires fewer staff).

The popularity of Spanish self-catering holidays has been growing rapidly. Ten years ago less than a third of package holidaymakers self-catered – now the proportion of self-catering to hotels is about half and half. The success of self-catering is easy to explain: price. For families on a tight budget, buying a self-catering package is the only option.

Most of the self-catering complexes in the major Spanish resorts offer basic but adequate standards of accommodation. For the price, they generally provide good value for money.

SPANISH *GITES?*

The one aspect of the market that has been slow to develop has been a Spanish equivalent to the French *gite* or the Tuscan farmhouse. Families who want to self-cater, but who don't fancy the tower-block complex have had little to choose from.

Over the past ten years as more and more British people have bought property on the Spanish Costas, there has been a big increase in the number of villas available. There is quite a wide variation in facilities and standard; most will have a pool but the furnishings are frequently no more than adequate. Of course, as in any purchase, you get what you pay for – but my experience suggests that in villa rentals, the Portuguese Algarve, for example, offers much better quality and much better value for money.

As well as trying the operators listed below, it's worth looking at the small ads in the main broadsheet Sunday newspapers. Another useful source of information is *Private Villas* magazine which lists a wide variety of private self-catering accommodation available for let in Spain. The magazine is bi-monthly and is sold at newsagents or can be obtained direct from the publishers, Private Villas Ltd (0564 794011).

Away from the seaside, sources of self-catering accommodation seem to be few and far between. The one area where this seems to be changing is northern Spain. Driven by the growth in ferry travel from the UK, operators seem to be developing this significant sector of the self-catering market.

As demand grows, it seems likely that inland Spain will emerge over the next few years as one of the key areas in the self-drive self-catering market. Could Navarra or Aragon become the new Dordogne and Gascony: if the price is right, clearly there is no shortage of people prepared to come on down.

Here is a guide to self-catering operators and the areas that they feature in their programme:

All over Spain

Airtours (0706 260000)
Destinations include Majorca, Minorca, Ibiza, the Canary Islands, Costa Brava, Costa Dorada, Costa Blanca, Costa del Sol and Costa de Almeria. For example, two weeks at the Andalucia Apartments in Benalmadena on the Costa del Sol costs from £234 to £389 per person, flight inclusive. This price is based on six persons sharing a two- or three-bedroom apartment.

Cosmosair (061 480 5799)
Destinations include the Balearic Islands, the Canary Islands, the Costa Brava, Costa Dorada, Costa Blanca, Costa de Almeria and the Costa del Sol. For example, fourteen nights at the Marvell Apartments in San Antonio on the island of Ibiza costs from £189 to £389 per person, based on four people sharing a one-bedroom apartment.

Mundi Color Holidays (071-828 6021)

As an example, Andalucia – one week in a two-bedroom villa in El Capistrano, Nerja, costs from £264 per person, including flights and Avis car hire. Mundi Color features the whole of Spain.

Portland Holidays (071-388 5111)

Destinations include the Canary Islands, Majorca, Ibiza, the Costa Blanca and Costa de Almeria. For example, two weeks at the Parque Santiago Apartments on the Playa de las Americas on the island of Tenerife costs from £229 to £359 per person, based on five sharing a two-bedroom apartment.

Thomson Holidays (021 632 6282)

Thomson's Summer Sun and Skytours brochures offer a range of good value, family units. For example, seven nights at the Mexico Apartments on the Costa Brava costs from £99 to £236 per adult, based on three sharing a studio. Self-catering in traditional villas is featured in the OSL brochure. For example, a villa in Pollensa, on Majorca, sleeping seven people costs from £239 to £462 per person.

Andalucia

CV Travel (071-581 0851)

Villas, houses and apartments in various parts of the region – Benahavis, Sotogrande, Estepona, Gaucin, La Almuna, Los Barrios and Aracena. Two weeks in a two-bedroom apartment at La Aldea, Benahavis costs from £385 to £570 per person, flight inclusive.

Individual Travellers Spain (07987 485)

Featuring the White Villages, a mixture of rural houses and villas with pools, including some near the coast at Estepona, at Arcos de la Frontera between Seville and Cadiz in the west and Granada and Almeria to the east. Prices range from £130 to £400 per person for one week, including return flights to Malaga.

Longwood Holidays (081-551 4494)

Marbella. Two weeks in a one-bedroom apartment costs from £428 to £663 per person, based on four people sharing. The price includes flights to Malaga and transfers.

Magic of Spain (081-748 7575)
Destinations featured include Nerja, Frigiliana, Gaucin, San Pedro, Costa de le Luz, Ronda and Mijas. Prices range from £313 to £920 per person for two weeks, including air fare to Malaga and car hire.

Meon Villa Holidays (0730 268411)
Destinations include Mijas, Fuengirola, Marbella, Estepona and San Pedro de Alcantara. Two weeks at a three-bedroom villa in Mijas costs from £389 to £740 per person, including flights and car hire.

Palmer & Parker Holidays (0494 815411)
Costa del Sol. For example, a villa in Marbella costs from £1240 to £5810 per week, including car hire. This price does not include air travel.

Portland Holidays (071-388 5111)
Costa de Almeria. Seven nights at the Macael Apartments costs from £149 to £250 per person, based on four sharing a one-bedroom apartment. Return air travel is included.

Rosemary & Frances Villas (071-235 8825)
A restored Spanish hacienda, sleeping up to seventeen people with a private pool and a paddle tennis court. The rental includes three residential staff. Escorted horseriding can be arranged. The property costs £8092 per week.

Spanish Affair (071-385 8127)
Apartments, villas and farmhouses – some with pools – sleeping from two to twelve people. For example, a two-week holiday in a villa in Caesares, sleeping six people and with its own pool costs from £332 to £572 per person, flight and car hire inclusive. Children aged two to eleven years get a £40 reduction.

Travellers' Way (0527 836791)
Coastal and inland cottages, bungalows, apartments and luxury villas. For example, a country house with its own swimming pool, near Montejaque sleeping six people costs from £395 to £475 per week. This price does not include air travel.

Ultimate Holidays (0279 755527)
Costa del Sol. Destinations include Fuengirola. For example, two weeks at the Pyr Studio costs from £219 to £425 per person, based on four sharing a one-bedroom apartment. Prices include air travel.

Balearic Islands

Beach Villas Holidays (0223 311113)
Majorca. The main programme is based in the north of Majorca in the resorts of Puerto Pollensa, Alcudia and San Vincente. A mixture of private villas with pools and apartments is offered. For example, two weeks in a villa costs from £344 to £501 per person, air inclusive.

CV Travel (071-581 0851)
Majorca. Villas in Puerto Pollensa, the Vall d'en March, La Font and Santa Maria. Two weeks in a villa near Pollensa, sleeping seven people, costs from £300 to £480 per person, flight inclusive. *Minorca.* One villa at San Clemente sleeping eight people costs from £1035 to £1925 per week, villa rental only.

Celtic Holidays (0622 690009)
Villa and apartment holidays on the island of Minorca. For example, a three-bedroom villa with its own pool costs from £195 to £325 per person for one week, based on six people sharing, flight inclusive.

Club Pollensa Holidays (0903 200237)
Countryside villas with pools and apartments in Puerto Pollensa and Cala San Vincente in Majorca. For example, a two-bedroom villa, sleeping up to six people, close to the old town of Pollensa, with its own pool, costs from £335 to £725 per week. Flights and car hire are extra.

European Villas (0223 314220)
Ibiza. Resorts include C'an Germa, San Agustin, Cala Tarida, C'an Tumas, Cala Moli, Cala Vadella and Cala Carbo. Two weeks at a three-bedroom villa costs from £295 to £550 per person, including return air fare. *Majorca.* Resorts featured are Cas Concos and S'Horta. Two weeks at a three-bedroomed villa costs from £245 to £480 per person, including return air

fare. *Minorca*. Resorts featured are Cala Galdana, Cala'n Bosch and Cala Blanca. Two weeks at a three-bedroom villa costs from £240 to £505 per person, including return air fare.

Iberotravel (0532 393020)
Destinations include Puerto Pollensa and Cala d'Or in Majorca and Cala'n Porter in Minorca. For example, a three-bedroom villa with pool and free car in the Puerto Pollensa area costs from £329 to £579 per person for two weeks.

Individual Travellers Spain (07987 485)
Majorca. Mostly in the unspoilt, mountainous region around Pollensa in the north, as well as some less well-known inland locations. Mainly private villas with pools, some beach-front apartments. Prices range from £180 to £350 per person for one week, including return flights to Palma. *Minorca*. A handful of traditional houses on this unspoilt, quiet island. Prices range from £155 to £345 per person for one week, including return flights to Mahon.

Magic of Spain (081-748 7575)
Majorca. Destinations include Puerto Pollensa, Cala Figuera and Valldemossa. Prices range from £330 to £1121 per person for two weeks, including air fare to Palma and car hire.

Majorca Farmhouse Holidays (0734 462181)
For example, a four-bedroom, luxurious house in the mountains above the bay of Puerto Pollensa costs from £750 to £1975 per week. This price does not include air travel.

Meon Villa Holidays (0730 268411)
Minorca, Majorca and Ibiza. For example, two weeks at a three-bedroom villa on Minorca costs from £431 to £987 per person, including flights and car hire.

PCI Holidays (0444 440606)
Minorca. Villas and apartments from £185 to £335 per week for a two-bedroom apartment outside Mahon. This price does not include travel.

Panorama Holiday Group (0273 206531)
Apartments in Ibiza and Majorca. For example, seven nights self-catering at the Zodiac Apartments in Es Cana, Ibiza costs from £189 to £299 per person, based on four people sharing. This price includes air travel.

Patricia Wildblood (081-658 6722)
Minorca. For example, two weeks in a modern villa by the sea at Cala Santa Galdana with a pool, barbecue and garden table tennis costs from £380 to £665 per person, based on eight sharing, flight inclusive.

Secret Spain (0449 737664)
Majorca, near Pollensa. For example, a two-week holiday in a converted farmhouse, sleeping six people costs from £115 to £265 per person, accommodation only.

Speedwing (081-905 5252)
Majorca, Ibiza and Minorca. For example, a two-week package in a villa in Pollensa costs from £251 to £1091 per person, including return flights and a free Group B hire car.

Style Holidays (081-568 1999)
Minorca. Private villas with pools and apartments. A fourteen-night holiday at the three-bedroom Villa Binibel, sleeping six people, with its own private pool costs from £259 to £449 per person, flight inclusive. Rental only deals are available.

The Travel Club of Upminster (0708 225000)
From studios to luxury villas in northern Majorca and Minorca. Two weeks at a three-bedroom villa with pool ranges from £368 to £494 per person, with a minimum of five people. A one-bedroom studio with a shared pool for two weeks ranges from £368 to £488 per person with a minimum of two adults – with two children up to nineteen years of age at half price (including during school holidays). All prices include air travel.

The Villa Club (0223 311322)
Ibiza. Resorts include C'an Germa, San Agustin, Cala Tarida, C'an Tumas, Cala Moli, Cala Vadella and Cala Carbo. Two weeks at a three-bedroom villa costs from £295 to £550 per person, including air fare. *Majorca.* Resorts featured are Cas

Concos, Cala Ferrera, Cala d'Or, Son Carrio and Porto Colom. Two weeks at a two-bedroom apartment costs from £220 to £369 per person, including return air fare. *Minorca.* Resorts featured are Cala Galdana, Cala'n Bosch, Cala Blanes and Cala Blanca. Two weeks at a three-bedroom bungalow costs from £215 to £370 per person, including return air fare.

Ultimate Holidays (0279 755527)
Majorca and Minorca. Destinations include Santa Ponsa, Palma Nova and Cala 'n Porter. For example, two weeks at the Holiday Centre Apartments in Santa Ponsa cost from £179 to £375 per person, based on four sharing a one-bedroom apartment. Prices include air travel.

Villa Select (0789 764909)
Cala D'Or and Pollensa in Majorca and Minorca. For example, a two-bedroom villa, sleeping four people near the old town of Pollensa costs from £350 to £750 per week. This price does not include air travel.

Vintage Spain (0954 261431)
Majorca. Destinations featured include Pollensa, Puerto Pollensa and Sa Pobla in the north and S'Horta, C'As Concos and Porto Colom in the south-east. Traditional farmhouses accommodate from four to twelve people and range from £256 per person in low season to £523 per person in the high season for two weeks, including the return air fare to Palma. Rental only varies from £275 to £1455 weekly.

Canary Islands

Allegro Holidays (0444 248222)
Apartments on Tenerife, Lanzarote and Gran Canaria. Seven-day holidays start from £199 per person, air inclusive.

Beach Villas Holidays (0223 311113)
A mixture of private apartments and villas in Lanzarote, Gran Canaria and Tenerife. Prices range from £284 to £407 per person for two weeks, air inclusive.

Corona Holidays of London (081-530 2500)

Bungalows, apartments and villas on Gran Canaria, Fuerteventura, Lanzarote, Tenerife, La Gomera, El Hierro and La Palma. For example, an apartment in Playa Calera on the island of La Gomera costs from £7.55 to £9.95 per person per night, based on four sharing.

Flightline (0782 639833)

Apartments very near the beach are offered on Lanzarote and Tenerife. Prices on request.

H20 Holidays (0273 819999)

Apartments and bungalows in Lanzarote, Tenerife and Fuerteventura. For example, a two-bedroom beach apartment in Puerto del Carmen costs from £199 to £259 per person, per week, based on four people sharing. This price includes air travel.

Inspirations Holidays (0293 822244)

Tenerife, Gran Canaria and Lanzarote. For example, fourteen nights self-catering at the Xanadu Apartments near Playa de las Americas on the island of Tenerife, costs from £195 to £361 per person, based on four sharing. This price includes air travel.

Islands in the Sun (0920 484515)

Lanzarote and Fuerteventura. For example, one week's holiday in a one-bedroom bungalow, sleeping two people near Corralejo, Fuerteventura, costs from £239 to £344 per person, flight inclusive.

James Villa Holidays (0732 840846)

Apartments and villas on the islands of Lanzarote, Tenerife, Fuerteventura and Gran Canaria. For example, a bungalow sleeping four people in Puerto del Carmen on the island of Lanzarote costs from £319 to £359 per property, per week.

Lanzarote Leisure (081-449 7441)

Lanzarote, Fuerteventura and Tenerife. For example, a three-bedroom villa sleeping five people, near the coastal resort of Callao Salvaje on the island of Tenerife, costs from £192 to £348 per person for one week, flight inclusive.

Meon Villa Holidays (0730 268411)
Lanzarote. Two weeks at a three-bedroom villa costs from £443 to £787 per person, including flights and car hire.

Prestige Holidays (0425 480400)
Apartments in Lanzarote and bungalows in Gran Canaria. For example, seven nights in a two-bedroom bungalow in Gran Canaria, sleeping five guests costs from £279 to £349 per person, flight inclusive.

Rosemary & Frances Villas (071-235 8825)
Lanzarote: the property consists of a main villa, two separate apartments, a swimming pool patio area and a poolside shower. It is situated at the edge of the village of Guime on the south side of the island. The property costs £1580 per week.

Ultimate Holidays (0279 755527)
Tenerife and Lanzarote. Destinations include Playa de las Americas, Puerto del Carmen and Playa los Pocillos. For example, two weeks at the La Penita Apartments in Puerto del Carmen costs from £259 to £399 per person, based on four sharing a one-bedroom apartment. Prices include air travel.

Villa Select (0789 764909)
Tenerife and Lanzarote. For example, a three-bedroom villa, sleeping six people with a private pool in Puerto De Santiago on the southernmost tip of Tenerife costs from £975 to £995 per week. This price does not include air travel.

Villanza (0245 262496)
Villa and apartment holidays on Lanzarote and Fuerteventura. For example, a three/four-bedroom property with its own pool, in Puerto del Carmen costs from £169 to £344 per person, per week, based on six people sharing, flight inclusive.

Cantabria/Asturias

Brittany Ferries (0705 827701)
Seaside apartments and country *casas.* Two weeks at a one-bedroom house in Cerrazo near Santillana costs from £284 per person. A seaside apartment for up to five adults at Llanes

costs up to £814 per person for the first two people and £183 for each extra adult.

Casas Cantabricas (0223 328721)
Properties in areas south of Santander, Comillas, Cabezon de la Sal, San Vincente de la Barquera and Potes. Two weeks (based on a family of four), including accommodation and direct car ferry from the UK to northern Spain (Brittany Ferries or P&O) costs on average £260 to £375 per person.

Secret Spain (0449 737664)
Eastern Asturias. Typical homes, some in walking distance of the beaches, some in the foothills of the Picos mountains. For example, two weeks in a simple mountain house sleeping up to six people, for a family of four with a car costs from £235 to £395 per person. This price includes return ferry travel from Portsmouth to Bilbao with cabin accommodation.

Spantrek (0457 836250)
All properties are based in the Picos de Europa mountain range. They are mostly rural and two weeks in a house for five people costs between £570 and £750 – rental only.

Travellers' Way (0527 836791)
Country cottages in Asturias. For example, a four-bedroom farmhouse near Villaviciosa, set in its own grounds with fruit trees costs from £265 to £370 per week. Does not include travel.

Castille and Leon

Individual Travellers Spain (07987 485)
A handful of typical Spanish houses in the south of this region between Segovia and La Adrada within easy reach of Madrid. Prices range from £220 to £350 per person for one week, including return flights to Madrid.

Catalonia

Beach Villas Holidays (0223 311113)
Costa Brava. Predominantly apartments with a selection of private inland villas. Two weeks in an apartment costs from £190 to £347 per person, air inclusive.

Brittany Ferries (0705 827701)
Costa Brava: destinations include Playa de Pals. Two weeks in April/May start from £246 per person for the first two people occupying a three-bedroom apartment. Extra adults cost £113 each. The price increases to £892 per person in high season with extra adults costing £183 each.

European Villas (0223 314220)
Resorts featured are Casa de Campo, Tamariu, Bagur and Canyellas. Two weeks at a three-bedroom villa costs from £219 to £510 per person, including return air fare to Gerona.

Individual Travellers Spain (07987 485)
A selection of countryside houses near Figueras plus Cadaques – the birthplace of Salvador Dali. Prices range from £180 to £300 per person for one week, including return flights to Barcelona.

Magic of Spain (081-748 7575)
Destinations featured include the medieval village of Pals and the resort of Sitges. Prices range from £305 to £1039 per person for two weeks, including air fare to Barcelona.

PCI Holidays (0444 440606)
Apartments and villas in Pals, Sa Riera, Begur, Aigua Blava, Tamariu and Llafranc. A villa in Pals with two bedrooms and a swimming pool costs from £340 to £656 per week. This price does not include travel.

Prima Villas (0752 256678)
Traditional Spanish villas and modern houses – many with pools. Destinations featured include La Escala, Aigua Xelida, Aiguablava and Begur. Two weeks at La Escala in a traditional villa for eight people costs from £195 to £355 per person, including return air fare.

Spanish Harbour Holidays (0272 373759)
Destinations featured include Tamariu, Llafranch, Calella de Palafrugell, Sa Riera, Sa Tuna, L'Escala, Port De La Selva, Llanca and Aiguablava. For example, a two-bedroom apartment near the beach in Tamariu costs from £190 to £380 per person for two weeks, flight inclusive.

The Villa Club (0223 311322)
Costa Brava. Resorts featured are Calella, Llafranch, Aigua Blava, Pals, Estartit, Tamariu, Bagur and Canyellas. Two weeks at a two-bedroom apartment costs from £216 to £430 per person, including return air fare.

Vintage Spain (0954 261431)
Destinations featured include Begur, Palafrugell (Llafanch, Tamariu), Calonge, Pals and Vall Llobrega. Houses accommodate from four to fourteen people and prices range from £241 per person in low season to £653 per person in the high season for two weeks, including return air fare to Gerona. Rental only varies from £245 to £3250 weekly.

Galicia

Casas Cantabricas (0223 328721)
Properties along the coast between Laxe and Carnota. Two weeks (based on a family of four), including house accommodation and direct car ferry from the UK to northern Spain (Brittany Ferries or P&O) costs on average from £260 to £375 per person.

Secret Spain (0449 737664)
Rias Bajas. Houses and apartments near beaches. A two-week ferry-inclusive package in an apartment on the beach for a family of four costs from £242 to £421 per person.

Travellers' Way (0527 836791)
Houses near the beach in San Vincente and La Coruna. A two-bedroom house, sleeping four people, in the village of San Vincente costs from £270 to £375 per week. This price does not include air travel.

Murcia

Connexions (0444 417299)
Villas, studios and apartments within the La Manga Club which is located between the city of Murcia and Cartagena. The club is owned by P&O and managed by Hyatt Hotels. It extends over 1400 acres of land and is made up of three Andalucian-style villages. For example, seven nights at a three-bedroom villa at

Las Higueras which has air conditioning and its own splash pool and private gardens costs from £306 to £371 per person, flight inclusive. This price is for six people sharing.

Pyrenees

Travellers' Way (0527 836791)
Village houses in the Tremp Valley. For example, a recently renovated stone house with two bedrooms, sleeping four people, costs from £300 to £395 per week. This price does not include travel.

Valencia

Beach Villas Holidays (0223 311113)
Costa Blanca. A large programme of private villas with pools in Javea, Calpe and Moraira. Two weeks in a villa costs from £304 to £489 per person, air inclusive.

Brittany Ferries (0705 827701)
Destinations include Javea and Moraira. One week in a three-bedroom villa at Moraira in March costs from £301 per person for the first two people and £71 for each extra adult. Two weeks in Javea during late July costs £821 per person for the first two people and £124 each for any extra adults.

European Villas (0223 314220)
Costa Blanca. Resorts featured are Javea, Moraira and Denia. Two weeks at a three-bedroom villa costs from £250 to £480 per person, including return air fare to Alicante.

Individual Travellers Spain (07987 485)
A selection of villas, many with pools, between Valencia and Alicante, all within easy reach of the coast. Prices range from £144 to £300 per person for one week, including return flights to Alicante.

Magic of Spain (081-748 7575)
Costa Blanca. Destinations include Javea and Moraira. Prices range from £426 to £962 per person for two weeks, including air fare to Alicante and car hire.

Meon Villa Holidays (0730 268411)

Javea. Two weeks at a three bedroom villa costs from £394 to £634 per person, including flights and car hire.

Prima Villas (0752 256678)

Traditional and modern villas in Javea and the surrounding area. All have private pools. Two weeks in Javea in a traditional *finca* sleeping nine people, costs from £196 to £338 per person, including air fares.

Speedwing (081-905 5252)

Costa Blanca. Two-week packages from £251 to £965 per person, including villa, return flights and a free Group B hire car.

The Villa Club (0223 311322)

Costa Blanca. Resorts featured are Javea, Moraira and Denia. Two weeks at a three-bedroom villa costs from £208 to £390 per person, including air fare.

Travellers' Way (0527 836791)

Villas with pools on the Costa Blanca. A three-bedroom villa, sleeping six to seven people in Moraira, with its own swimming pool, costs from £325 to £575 per week. This price does not include air travel.

HOUSE SWAPPING

How to Swap

The most straightforward way to arrange an overseas or UK swap is to advertise, for a fee, in a house-swapping directory: the biggest is produced by Intervac. Several directories are published in Britain:

Home Base Holidays, 7 Park Avenue, London N13 5PG (081-886 8752): Specializes in home swaps with families in the US and Canada. It produces three brochures a year; membership costs £32.

Homelink International, Linfield House, Gorse Hill Road, Virginia Water, Surrey GU25 4AS (0344 842642): One of the biggest home-swapping agencies with more than 16,000 registered members in over fifty countries, it publishes six catalogues during the year; annual membership £47.

Intervac International Home Exchange, Orchard Court, North Wraxall, Chippenham, Wiltshire SN14 7AD (0225 892208): Over 9000 members and three directories a year (with a late-exchange service). Annual membership is £65.

You could also consider trying to arrange a swap through personal contacts: friends or friends of friends who live overseas. If the company you work for, for example, has overseas offices and representatives, perhaps you might be able to organize a swap through them.

The Possible Dangers

According to the home-swapping agencies, home-swapping disasters hardly ever happen: the only problem is likely to be that the person you're planning to swap with has to back out because of family illness or the death of a relative.

The agencies report that families are very good about paying for any breakages or any damage they cause. Intervac says the fact that there is no rental fee involved seems to make people especially careful about how they treat the house where they are unminded guests. But if you are especially houseproud house swapping may not suit you. If you wish to swap your house, it helps if it is in a place well known as a tourist area: in London, for example, or Oxford – but location isn't always important.

Insurance: You must tell your house and car insurance company about the exchange: if you don't, it may affect your cover.

Further information: The Consumers Association magazine *Which?* (November 1986) has a very useful guide to house swapping, and advice on making the necessary arrangements. Back numbers of *Which?* are available from reference libraries.

5

HOTELS AND PARADORS

THE INDEPENDENT TRAVELLER IS PENALIZED

The Spanish hotel industry largely exists to accommodate the needs of overseas tour operating business. There are Spanish hotel chains but unlike, say, Forte or Hilton, they are generally not used to people turning up at their reception desk without either a booking or a tour operator's voucher.

Incredibly, the person with the nous to turn up at a hotel on his own initiative is likely to be charged dearly for his business. While these hotel chains offer cut-to-the-bone prices to tour operators, they appear to have no similar facility for dealing with ordinary members of the public keen to put together their own package.

This will have to change. As ways of selling holidays change through the advent of new technology, Spanish hotel groups will have to direct more of their sales and marketing effort to dealing with the consumer direct.

At the moment, however, the prospective do-it-yourself holidaymaker tends to be offered no special treatment, as far as price is concerned. But it's always worth asking for a deal. Write – or better still, fax – and ask them for a discount: they can only say no.

Alternatively consider making a booking through a hotel reservation agency such as Hotels Abroad (0689 857838); HPS (081-446 0126) and Room Service (071-636 6888).

Local tourist boards in Spain are also becoming more active in handling hotel bookings. For example, the Majorca Tourist Board has set up a Hotel Reservations Centre in Palma (010 34 71 208 459) to take bookings for what it calls 'hotels of character' and 'rural retreats'.

Paradors

Spain's best-known hotel chain – the government-owned network of Paradors – was established in the 1920s to provide good accommodation in those places that lacked decent hotels. 'Parador' in Spanish means literally a 'stopping place', a rather inelegant name you might have thought, for what are frequently quite magnificent establishments where you are offered an experience rather more marvellous than merely a 'stopping off' place en route to somewhere else.

There are now more than eighty Paradors situated all over Spain, and more than a third of them are to be found in castles, former convents and other ancient monuments or places of historic interest.

If the hotel isn't beautiful in itself – a number of Paradors are sadly modern and plug-ugly (although others are modern and handsomely built in traditional style) – they will be in places of outstanding natural beauty. A striking percentage are not only beautiful buildings but are also in beautiful locations (see the Hotel Los Reyes Catolicos in Santiago, for example, or the Hostal San Marcos in Leon).

Many Paradors are sumptuously furnished with tapestries, antique furniture and period paintings – and virtually all are decorated and furnished in traditional style – even if newly built. You can expect the bedrooms to be comfortably furnished and spacious, with a big bath and giant bath-towels to match.

The Paradors are not perfect, though. About five years ago, you could expect to spend around £30 per room per night in a Parador. Now the average price is at least twice that amount.

And service in the Paradors is not always all that it might be. They are, after all, state-owned (imagine a hotel run by the Co-Op!). Reception staff often lack interpersonal skills, for example (i.e. they can be downright rude!). But for the most part, a night in a Parador will be a Night to Remember! Paradors are generally welcoming to children (like every other Spanish place).

Parador bookings in the UK through Keytel International (071-402 8182) which can supply a full directory and a Parador map.

WHERE TO FIND THE PARADORS

The quotes are from the Spanish tourist office Paradors brochure. 's/n' stands for *sin nombre* – no street number.

Andalucia

Parador de Antequera, 29200 Antequera (Malaga): 'Modern-built parador in historical town.'
Tel: 95 284 02 61 Fax: 95 284 13 12

Parador de Arcos de la Frontera, Plaza de Espana, 11630 Arcos de la Frontera (Cadiz): 'Modern building on a sharp ridge with panoramic views.'
Tel: 956 70 05 00 Fax: 956 70 11 16

Parador de Ayamonte, El Castillito, 21400 Ayamonte (Huelva): 'Modern building overlooking the city of Ayamonte with magnificent views of the Guadiana river.'
Tel: 959 32 07 00 Fax: 959 32 07 00

Parador de Bailen, Avenida de Malaga s/n, 23710, Bailen (Jaen): 'Modern-built hotel close to the narrow pass of Despenaperros.'
Tel: 953 67 01 00 Fax: 953 67 25 30

Hotel 'Atlantico' Cadiz, Duque de Najera 9, 11002 Cadiz: 'Modern hotel at the end of the Genoves park facing the sea in one of the city's most splendid settings.'
Tel: 956 22 69 05 Fax: 956 21 45 82

Parador de Carmona, 41410 Carmona (Sevilla): 'Situated among the remains of the Arriba fortress built by the Moors.'
Tel: 95 414 10 10 Fax: 95 414 17 12

Parador de Cazorla, 23470 Cazorla (Jaen): 'Built in typical Andalucia farmhouse style set in the mountainous Sierra de Cazorla.'
Tel: 953 72 10 75 Fax: 953 72 10 75

Parador de Cordoba, Avda de la Arruzafa s/n, 14012 Cordoba: 'Modern building at the foot of the Sierra Cordobesa.'
Tel: 957 27 59 00 Fax: 957 28 04 09

Parador de Granada, Alhambra, 18009 Granada: 'In a former Franciscan convent within the Alhambra complex with magnificent views.'
Tel: 958 22 14 40 Fax: 958 22 22 64

Parador de Jaen, 23001 Jaen: 'On top of Mount Santa Catalina, next to the ruins of the Moorish fortress built by the same ruler responsible for Granada's Alhambra.'
Tel: 953 23 00 00 Fax: 953 23 09 30

Parador de Malaga-Del Golf, Aptdo de correos 324, 29080 Malaga: 'Modern seaside hotel with a golf course, well placed for exploring the western Costa del Sol and nearby town of Ronda.'
Tel: 95 238 12 55 Fax: 95 238 21 41

Parador de Malaga-Gibralfaro, 29016 Malaga: 'Traditional-style building situated on Gibralfaro Mountain next to the Moorish fortress, with magnificent views over the bay and of the city.'
Tel: 95 222 19 03 Fax: 95 222 19 04

Parador de Mazagon, 21130 Mazagon (Huelva): 'Modern building surrounded by pine trees set on the ridge of a sandy cliff overlooking Mazagon beach.'
Tel: 959 53 63 00 Fax: 959 53 62 28

Parador de Mojacar, 04638 Mojacar (Almeria): 'Modern building on the Almeria coast near the beach.'
Tel: 950 47 82 50 Fax: 950 47 81 83

Parador de Nerja, 29780 Nerja (Malaga): 'Modern hotel located in the most attractive locations on the eastern Costa del Sol, near to the Balcony of Europe scenic viewpoint.'
Tel: 95 252 00 50 Fax: 95 252 19 97

Parador de Ubeda, Plaza de Vasquez Molina s/n, 23400 Ubeda (Jaen): 'Housed in a sixteenth-century palace in the historic

part of the city and one of the finest examples of Andalucian Renaissance architecture.'
Tel: 953 75 03 45 Fax: 953 75 12 59

Aragon

Parador de Alcaniz, Castillo de Calatravos, 44600 Alcaniz (Teruel): 'Convent-castle on a promontory in the middle of the city.'
Tel: 978 83 04 00 Fax: 978 83 03 66

Parador de Teruel, 44080 Teruel: 'Modern building well placed for excursions into the countryside of the Sierra de Albarracin, the Sierra de Gudar and the Puerta de Ademuz.'
Tel: 978 60 18 00 Fax: 978 60 86 12

North-west Spain

Parador de Bayona, Ctra de Bayona, Km 1.6, 36300 Bayona (Pontevedra): 'Building in the style of a Galician country manor house on a small peninsula with panoramic views.'
Tel: 986 35 50 00 Fax: 986 35 50 76

Parador de Cambados, Paseo de Cervantes s/n, 36630 Cambados (Pontevedra): 'In the ancient Pazo de Bazan, a nobleman's house.'
Tel: 986 54 22 50 Fax: 986 54 20 68

Parador de Ferrol, Almirante Fernandez Martin s/n, 15401 Ferrol (La Coruna): 'Traditional building in a busy sea port.'
Tel: 981 35 67 20 Fax: 981 35 67 20

Parador de Pontevedra, C/Baron 19, 36002 Pontevedra: 'In the old Pazo de Maceda – built in the style of a Galician country house – which is constructed over a Roman villa.'
Tel: 986 85 58 00 Fax: 986 85 21 95

Parador de Ribadeo, Amador Fernandez s/n, 27700, Ribadeo (Lugo): 'Traditional-style building with magnificent views of the Ribadeo estuary.'
Tel: 962 11 08 25 Fax: 962 11 03 46

Parador de Puebla de Sanabria, 49300 Puebla de Sanabria (Zamora): 'Modern-built hotel to the north-east of Zamora near the border with Portugal.'
Tel: 980 62 00 01 Fax: 980 62 03 51

Santiago de Compostela: Hotel Reyes Catolicos, Plaza del Obradoiro 1, 15705 Santiago de Compostela (La Coruna): 'Historical building originally the Royal Hospice founded for lodging pilgrims. It is claimed to be the oldest hotel in the world.'
Tel: 981 58 22 00 Fax: 981 56 30 94

Parador de Tuy, 36700 Tuy (Pontevedra): 'Traditional-style building standing on a promontory on the right bank of the river Mino near the Portuguese border.'
Tel: 986 60 03 09 Fax: 986 60 21 63

Parador de Verin, 32600 Verin (Orense): 'Situated next to the fortress of Monterrey, an impressive medieval castle.'
Tel: 988 41 00 75 Fax: 988 41 20 17

Parador de Villafranca del Bierzo, Avda de Calvo Sotelo s/n, 2500 Villafranca del Bierzo (Leon): 'Modern hotel in an attractive town on the old Pilgrims' Way.'
Tel: 987 54 01 75 Fax: 987 54 00 10

Parador de Villalba, Valeriano Valdesuso s/n, 27800 Villalba (Lugo): 'A small hotel – just six rooms – housed in an extraordinary octagonal Medieval fortress complete with drawbridge.'
Tel: 982 51 00 11 Fax: 982 51 00 90

Northern Spain

Parador de Cervera de Pisuerga, 34840 Cervera de Pisuerga (Palencia): 'Modern building in a peaceful site overlooking the Picos de Europa.'
Tel: 979 87 00 75 Fax: 979 87 01 05

Parador de Fuente De, 39588 Fuente De (Cantabria): 'Modern hotel in the valley of Liebana at the foot of the central and eastern Picos de Europa mountains.'
Tel: 942 73 66 51 Fax: 942 73 66 54

Parador de Gijon, Parrque de Isabel Catolica s/n, 33203 Gijon (Asturias): 'In a traditional-style building facing the sea.'
Tel: 98 537 05 11 Fax: 98 537 02 33

Parador de Santillana Del Mar, Plaza Ramon Pelayo 8, 39330 Santillana Del Mar (Cantabria): 'In a fifteenth-century building in the heart of a magnificent medieval town.'
Tel: 942 81 80 00 Fax: 942 81 83 91

North-east Spain

Parador de Argomaniz, Ctra N-1 Km 363, 01192 Argomaniz (Alava): 'Housed in the Renaissance Palacio de Larrea in a unique area of countryside called La Llanada Alavesa.'
Tel: 945 29 32 00 Fax: 945 29 32 87

Parador de Calahorra, Parque Era Alta s/n, 26500, Calahorra (La Rioja): 'Modern building located in the old Roman Calagurris.'
Tel: 941 13 03 58 Fax: 941 13 51 39

Parador de Hondarribia, Plaza de Armas 14, Hondarribia (Guipuzcoa): 'Housed in historic castle used by Charles V.'
Tel: 043 64 55 00 Fax: 943 64 21 53

Parador de Olite, Plaza de los Teobaldos 2, 31390 Olite (Navarra): 'Housed in a medieval castle where Carlos III spent the last years of his life.'
Tel: 948 74 00 00 Fax: 948 74 02 01

Parador de Santo Domingo de la Calzada, Plaza del Santo 3, 26250 Santo Domingo de la Calzada (La Rioja): 'On the site of old Pilgrims' Hospital in a fine historic city.'
Tel: 941 34 03 00 Fax: 941 34 03 25

Parador de Sos del Rey Catolico, 50680 Sos del Rey Catolico (Zaragoza): 'Situated on the medieval walls of an ancient town with a wealth of historical monuments.'
Tel: 948 88 80 11 Fax: 948 88 81 00

Catalonia and Costa Brava

Parador de Aiguablava, 17255 Bagur (Gerona): 'Modern functional building with splendid views of the Costa Brava.'
Tel: 972 62 21 62 Fax: 972 62 21 66

Parador de Cardona, 08261 Cardona (Barcelona): 'Situated in an eighth-century fortress on a high hill overlooking the river.'
Tel: 93 869 12 75 Fax: 93 869 16 36

Parador de Tortosa, 43500 Tortosa (Tarragona): 'Housed in the castle of La Zuda, on a hill overlooking the town.'
Tel: 977 44 44 50 Fax: 977 44 44 58

Parador de Vic, 08500 Vic (Barcelona): 'Built in the style of a Catalan farmhouse, overlooking a large reservoir.'
Tel: 93 812 23 23 Fax: 93 812 23 68

Pyrenees

Parador de Arties, 255999 Arties (Lleida): 'Traditional Parador – housed in one of the most historical and ancient buildings of the Aran Valley – in one of the most beautiful regions of the Catalan Pyrenees.'
Tel: 973 64 08 01 Fax: 973 64 10 01

Parador de Bielsa, Valle de Pineta, 22350, Bielsa (Huesca): 'Traditional-style building at the far end of the Pineta Valley, well-placed for visits to Ordesa National Park.'
Tel: 974 50 10 11 Fax: 974 60 11 88

Parador de Seo de Urgel, 25700 Seo de Urgel (Lleida): 'On the site of the old Santo Domingo church and convent, the hotel incorporates the courtyard and restored chapel.'
Tel: 973 35 20 00 Fax: 973 35 23 09

Parador de Viella, 25530 Viella (Lleida): 'Pyrenean-style building set in a spectacular circle of mountains in the Valle de Aran.'
Tel: 973 64 01 00 Fax: 973 64 11 00

Castile and Leon

Parador de Benavente, 49600 Benavente (Zamora): 'Housed in a huge twelfth-century castle still with its original tower.'
Tel: 980 63 03 00 Fax: 980 63 03 03

Parador de Ciudad Rodrigo, Plaza del Castillo 1, 37500 Ciudad Rodrigo (Salamanca): 'Housed in a fortress-castle on the banks of the Agueda river on a raised hill.'
Tel: 923 46 01 50 Fax: 923 46 04 04

Hotel San Marcos, Plaza de San Marcos 7, 24001 Leon: 'Historic building that once served as a resting place for pilgrims travelling to Santiago.'
Tel: 987 23 73 00 Fax: 987 23 34 58

Parador de Salamanca, Teso de la Feria 2, 37008 Salamanca: 'Modern building on the left bank of the Tormes river with magnificent views.'
Tel: 923 26 87 00 Fax: 923 21 54 38

Parador de Soria, Parque del Castillo, 42005 Soria: 'Located in the Parque del Castillo in a hilltop position with panoramic views of the surrounding countryside.'
Tel: 975 21 34 45 Fax: 975 21 28 49

Parador de Tordesillas, 47100 Tordesillas: 'Near the historic town of Tordesillas in a spacious garden surrounded by a pine wood.'
Tel: 983 77 00 51 Fax: 983 77 10 13

Parador de Zamora, Plaza de Viriato 5, 49001 Zamora: 'In a Renaissance palace built on the ruins of the alcazaba.'
Tel: 980 51 44 97 Fax: 980 53 00 63

Extremadura and New Castile

Parador de Alarcon, Avda Amigos de Castillos 3, 16213 Alarcon (Cuenca): 'Eighth-century fortress in a fortified town of Arab origin on an enormous rocky ridge.'
Tel: 969 33 13 50 Fax: 969 33 11 07

Parador de Albacete, CN-301, Km 251, 02000 Albacete: 'Recently built Parador in a town with an impressive archaeological museum.'
Tel: 967 50 93 43 Fax: 967 22 60 92

Parador de Almagrio, 13270 Almagrio (Ciudad Real): 'Built on the old Franciscan convent of Santa Catalina.'
Tel: 926 86 01 00 Fax: 926 86 01 50

Parador de Caceres, Calle Ancha 6, 10003 Caceres: 'Situated in the Palacio del Comendador in a town surrounded by Roman walls.'
Tel: 927 21 17 59 Fax: 927 21 17 29

Parador de Cuenca, Paseo Hoz del Huecar s/n, 16001 Cuenca: 'Located in the Convent of San Pablo, founded in 1523, in a place of great natural beauty overlooking the famous Hanging Houses.'
Tel: 969 23 23 20 Fax: 969 23 25 34

Parador de Guadalupe, Marques de la Romana 12, 10140 Guadalupe (Caceres): 'In a fifteenth-century building opposite the Guadalupe monastery and the pre-Roman ruins of Logrosan.'
Tel: 927 36 70 75 Fax: 927 36 70 76

Parador de Jarandilla de la Vera, 10450 Jarandilla de la Vera (Caceres): 'In an old castle built during the end of the fourteenth century: near the cathedral of Palencia and the villages of La Vera.'
Tel: 927 56 01 17 Fax: 927 56 00 88

Parador de Manzanares, 13200 Manzanares (Ciudad Real): 'Modern building well-placed for exploring La Mancha in the footsteps of Don Quijote.'
Tel: 926 61 04 00 Fax: 926 61 09 35

Parador de Merida, Plaza de la Constitucion 3, 06800 Merida (Badajoz): 'Housed in a building that was formerly a Roman temple, Visigoth Basilica and also an eighteenth-century convent. Merida has a wide array of Roman and Arab archaeological treasures.'
Tel: 924 31 38 00 Fax: 924 31 92 08

Parador de Oropesa, Plaza de Palacio 1, 45560 Oropesa (Toledo): 'In a palace that was once the residence of the Counts of Oropesa. The castle dates back to the Mohammedan era.'
Tel: 925 43 00 00 Fax: 925 43 07 77

Parador de Trujillo, Santa Beatriz de Silva 1, 10200 Trujillo (Caceres): 'Located in the convent of Santa Clara, situated among the medieval and Renaissance monuments of the town.'
Tel: 927 32 13 50 Fax: 927 32 13 66

Parador de Zafra, Plaza Corazon de Maria 7, 06300 Zafra (Badajoz): 'In a handsome castle which belonged to the Dukes of Feria: the building is famous for its Renaissance-style courtyard with Doric and Ionic columns.'
Tel: 924 55 45 40 Fax: 924 55 10 18

Madrid and Surrounding Region

Parador de Avila, Marques Canales de Chozas 2, 05001 Avila: 'Housed in sixteenth-century palace alongside the convent of the Encarnacion which was the birthplace of Santa Teresa.'
Tel: 920 21 13 40 Fax: 920 22 61 66

Parador de Chinchon, Avda Generalisimo 1, 28370 Chinchon (Madrid): 'Traditional-style building on the site of old Augustinian convent.'
Tel: 91 894 08 36 Fax: 91 894 09 08

Parador de Gredos, 05132 Gredos (Avila): 'The first Parador in the chain built in 1928 in a site personally selected by King Alfonso XIII. Well-placed for excursions into the Sierra de Gredos.'
Tel: 920 34 80 48 Fax: 920 34 82 05

Parador de Segovia, 40000 Segovia: 'Modern hotel with panoramic views of Segovia with its famous Roman aqueduct.'
Tel: 921 44 37 37 Fax: 921 43 73 62

Parador de Siguenza, Plaza del Castillo s/n, 19250 Siguenza (Guadalajara): 'Housed in what was originally a Visigoth castle but which later became a Moorish citadel.'
Tel: 949 39 01 00 Fax: 949 39 13 64

Parador de Toledo, Carro del Emperador s/n, 45002 Toledo: 'Toledo-style building located in the Los Cigarales area with striking views of the city.'
Tel: 925 22 18 50 Fax: 925 22 51 66

Valencia and Murcia

Parador de Benicarlo, Avda Papa Luna 3, 12580 Benicarlo (Castellon): 'Modern Parador next to the sea ideal for visiting the Costa del Azahar.'
Tel: 964 47 01 00 Fax: 964 47 09 34

Parador de Javea, 03730 Javea (Alicante): 'Modern hotel on a promontory next to El Arenal de Javea beach.'
Tel: 96 579 02 00 Fax: 96 579 03 08

Parador de Puerto Lumbreras, Avda Juan Carlos 1, 30890 Puerto Lumbreras (Murcia): 'Modern building well-placed for visits to the baroque town of Murcia.'
Tel: 968 40 20 25 Fax: 968 40 28 36

Parador de El Saler, 46012 El Saler (Valencia): 'Modern hotel near the sea, convenient for visits to Valencia.'
Tel: 96 161 11 86 Fax: 96 162 70 16

Canary Islands

Fuerteventura

Parador de Fuerteventura, Playa Blanca 35600 Puerto del Rosario, Isle de Fuerteventura (Las Palmas): 'Modern hotel on the east coast of the island of Fuerteventura.'
Tel: 928 85 11 50 Fax: 928 85 11 58

Gomera

Parador de San Sebastian de la Gomera, 38800 San Sebastian de la Gomera (Santa Cruz de Tenerife): 'Traditional nobleman's house surrounded by exotic gardens with panoramic views.'
Tel: 922 87 11 00 Fax: 922 87 11 16

Hierro

Parador de El Hierro, 38900 Isle de El Hierro (Santa Cruz de Tenerife): 'Modern building on the smallest of the Canary Islands.'
Tel: 922 55 80 36 Fax: 922 55 80 86

La Palma

Parador de Santa Cruz de la Palma, Avda Maritima 34, 38700 Santa Cruz de la Palma, Isla de La Palma (Santa Cruz de Tenerife): 'Canary Islands-style building facing the ocean in the heart of the city.'
Tel: 922 41 23 40 Fax: 922 41 18 56

Tenerife

Parador de Canadas del Teide, Aptdo Correos 15, Las Canadas del Teide, 38300 La Orotavia, Isla de Tenerife (Santa Cruz de Tenerife): 'Located a short distance from the foot of Mt Teide, Spain's highest point.'
Tel: 922 38 64 15 Fax: 922 38 64 15

AGROTURISMO

Like other European countries, Spain is developing the concept of agri-tourism: helping to sustain the countryside through tourism. The concept is most developed in Majorca where the local tourist board has produced a 'Countryside Stays' brochure which lists farmhouses and other old country buildings which have been converted to small up-market hotels with half-board accommodation available from around £40 per person per night.

Further information from Consorci per la Dinamitzacio Economica Al Medi Rural, Foners, 1-5E, 07006 Palma de Majorca (010 34 71 46 38 62).

Tour Operators Offering Special Hotel Packages

All over Spain

AA Driveaway (0256 493878)
Hotel touring holidays. Hotels and ferry crossings may be booked in advance or there is the option to book only the ferry and take nightly vouchers for your hotel accommodation. For example, one night at the three-star Novotel in Madrid costs from £75 to £123 per person on a bed and breakfast basis, based on two people sharing and including short sea ferry crossings. Extra nights cost from £27 per person.

Airtours (0706 260000)
Destinations include Majorca, Minorca, Ibiza, Tenerife, Gran Canaria, Lanzarote, Fuerteventura, Costa Brava, Costa Dorada, Costa Blanca, Costa Almeria and the Costa del Sol. For example, fourteen nights at the Hotel Nerja Club in Nerja on the Costa del Sol costs from £319 to £519 per person, flight inclusive and including half-board accommodation.

Cosmosair (061 480 5799)
Destinations include Majorca, Minorca, Ibiza, Tenerife, Gran Canaria, Lanzarote, Fuerteventura, Costa Brava, Costa Dorada, Costa Blanca, Costa Almeria, and the Costa del Sol. For example, fourteen nights at the three-star Hotel Panoramic in Alcudia on the island of Majorca on half board costs from £329 to £559 per person, flight inclusive.

Hotels Abroad (0689 857838)
En route and short-stay accommodation – mainly for motorists. For example, a one-night stay at a Posada near the Alhambra Palace in Granada costs around £30 per double room.

Mundi Color Holidays (071-828 6021)
Destinations throughout Spain, particularly featuring the quieter side of the popular summer holiday locations. For example, two weeks in Nerja, Costa del Sol costs from £550 to £756 per person. This includes return flights, Avis car hire and bed and breakfast accommodation.

Page & Moy (0533 524433)

Two- and three-centre holidays in Andalucia, Galicia, Madrid, Segovia, Toledo and Barcelona. For example, a ten-night holiday to Barcelona and the Orange Blossom coast costs from £499 to £529 per person. This price includes flights, seven nights' half board and three nights bed and breakfast accommodation.

Sovereign (0293 599988)

Destinations include Fuerteventura, Tenerife, Gran Canaria, Lanzarote, Majorca, Minorca, Ibiza and southern Spain. For example, fourteen nights at the three-star Hotel Rey Carlos III in Es Castell, Minorca, costs from £461 to £555 per person, flight inclusive and including bed and breakfast accommodation.

Thomson Holidays (021 632 6282)

Good value, family units and smaller hotels for those who prefer a quieter holiday. For example, seven nights' half board at the Hotel Taurus Park on the Costa Brava costs from £159 to £264 per person, fourteen nights bed and breakfast accommodation at the Hotel Carotti in Puerto Pollensa costs from £205 to £332 per person.

Andalucia

CV Travel (071-581 0851)

A selection of small properties in Carmona, Gaucin, Las Cabezas and Aracena. Usually sold as short breaks, from three to four nights up to one-week stays. Four nights at the Hacienda De San Rafael on half board costs from £394 to £455 per person, including flights to Seville.

Iberotravel (0532 393020)

Fuengirola, Costa del Sol. Two weeks at the Hotel Fuengirola Park costs from £345 to £515 per person, flight inclusive.

Kirker Holidays (071-231 3333)

Rural Andalucia. Family holidays to the Finca Buen Vino near Aracena, 70 km north of Seville. Staying *en famille* with an English family but in great comfort (private bathrooms, luxurious bedrooms, gourmet food and wine included). Alternatively, holidays to the exclusive Hacienda San Rafael,

63

set in the countryside amongst sunflower and cotton fields between Jerez and Seville. Great luxury – all inclusive (no extra charge for dinner, drinks, *tapas* or wine). Both holidays include flights and car hire. Individual quotations on request.

Longwood Holidays (081-551 4494)
A broad range of hotels is offered, from three-star in Torremolinos to five-star in Marbella. Seven nights at the El Fuerte Hotel in Marbella costs from £404 to £534 per person, based on two sharing. Seven nights at the Sol Patos in Benalmadena costs from £208 to £358 per person, based on two sharing. Prices include bed and breakfast accommodation, return flights to Malaga and transfers.

Magic of Spain (081-748 7575)
Costa del Sol, Costa de le Luz, Seville, Cordoba, Granada and *Cadiz*. Prices range from £435 to £2000 per person for two weeks, including flights from London.

Portland Holidays (071-388 5111)
Costa de Almeria. A seven-night half-board package at the Hotel Golf Trinidad costs from £214 to £339 per person, flight inclusive.

Travellers' Way (0527 836791)
Small hotels, country inns and beach hotels throughout the region. A stay at the Hotel Cortijo Fain in Arcos De la Frontera costs £40 per person, per night on a bed and breakfast basis. The ten-bedroom hotel is a converted farmhouse and is situated in an olive grove. It also has a swimming pool.

Ultimate Holidays (0279 755527)
Costa del Sol. Destinations featured include Benalmadena and Fuengirola. For example, a two-week half-board package to the Hotel Balmoral in Benalmadena costs from £289 to £445 per person, including air travel.

Balearic Islands

CV Travel (071-581 0851)
Majorca. Four nights at the Hotel Residencia in Deia ranges from £469 to £655 per person on a bed and breakfast basis, including flights to Palma.

Castaways (0737 812255)
Majorca. A seven-night half-board package at the Hotel Sa Coma, Banalbufar costs from £386 to £438 per person, including flights from Gatwick.

Celtic Holidays (0622 690009)
Three-star hotels on the island of Minorca. For example, a seven-night stay at the Hotel San Luis, in the resort of S'Algar, on half board costs from £305 to £415 per person, flight inclusive.

Classic Collection Holidays (0903 823088)
Hotels range from one-star to five-star and are located in coastal resorts, inland villages and mountain retreats. For example, seven nights' bed and breakfast in Palma at the Hotel Costa Azul costs from £267 per person, including scheduled flights and transfers.

Club Pollensa Holidays (0903 200237)
Puerto Pollensa and Cala San Vincente on the north coast of Majorca. For example, a week's stay at the three-star Illa D'Or in Puerto Pollensa costs from £242 to £295 per person, including half-board accommodation. This price does not include air travel.

Iberotravel (0532 393020)
Majorca, Minorca and Ibiza. For example, two weeks at the Hotel Punta Negra on the Costa d'en Blanes in Majorca costs from £899 to £1289 per person, flight inclusive. Alternatively two weeks at the Hotel Piscis in Alcudia, Majorca costs from £249 to £419 per person, flight inclusive.

Magic of Spain (081-748 7575)
Majorca. Destinations include Palma, Pollensa, Felanitx, Valldemossa, Deya and Santanyi. Prices range from £435 to £2000 per person for two weeks, including flights from London.

Majorca Farmhouse Holidays (0734 462181)
Hotels and guest houses mostly located in Puerto Pollensa and Cala San Vincente. For example, a week at the four-star Hotel Illa D'or overlooking the Puerto Pollensa Bay costs from £175

to £285 per person, per week on a half-board basis. This price does not include air travel.

Panorama Holiday Group (0273 206531)
Mostly two- and three-star hotels in Majorca and Ibiza. For example, seven nights' half board at the Hotel Ponent Playa in Cala D'Or in Majorca costs from £259 to £385 per person, flight inclusive.

Portland Holidays (071-388 5111)
Majorca and Ibiza. Two weeks at the Hotel Atlantic on the island of Ibiza costs from £242 to £399 per person, flight inclusive and including half-board accommodation.

The Travel Club of Upminster (0708 225000)
From four-star to one-star hotels in Majorca and Minorca. For example, two weeks' half-board accommodation at the four-star Santo Tomas in Minorca costs from £514 to £688 per person. Two weeks half-board accommodation at the three-star Hotel Daina in Puerto Pollensa in Majorca costs from £378 to £608 per person. All prices include air travel.

Ultimate Holidays (0279 755527)
Majorca. Destinations include Cala D'Or, Alcudia, Magalluf, Santa Ponsa, Costa De Calvia and Palma Nova. For example, a two-week half-board package to the Hotel Rocador in Cala D'Or costs from £395 to £555 per person including return air travel from London.
Minorca. Destinations featured include Cala 'n Blanes and Cala 'n Bosch. For example, a two-week half-board package to Hotel Cala 'n Blanes costs from £319 to £609 per person including return air travel from London.

Canary Islands

Allegro Holidays (0444 248222)
Tenerife, Lanzarote and Gran Canaria. Seven days at a three-star hotel on half board starts from £319 per person, air inclusive.

Corona Holidays of London (081-530 2500)
Accommodation is offered on the islands of La Palma, El Hierro and La Gomera. For example, a stay at the three-star

Maritimo Hotel in Santa Cruz de la Palma on the island of La Palma costs from £18.75 to £25.35 per person, per night, based on two people sharing.

Flightline (0782 639833)
Modern hotels in both quiet and lively locations on the islands of Lanzarote and Tenerife. Prices on application.

Iberotravel (0532 393020)
Destinations include Fuerteventura, Lanzarote and Tenerife. For example, two weeks at the Hotel Duna Park in Corralejo, Fuerteventura costs from £649 to £845 per person, flight inclusive.

Inspirations Holidays (0293 822244)
Tenerife, Gran Canaria and Lanzarote. For example, seven nights' half-board accommodation at the Eugenia Victoria Hotel on the island of Gran Canaria costs from £290 to £444 per person, flight inclusive.

Portland Holidays (071-388 5111)
Tenerife, Gran Canaria, Lanzarote and Fuerteventura. For example, two weeks' half board at the Hotel Sol Parque on the island of Tenerife costs from £383 to £505 per person, flight inclusive.

Prestige Holidays (0425 480400)
Four- and five-star hotels in Lanzarote, Tenerife, Gran Canaria and Fuerteventura. For example, fourteen nights at the five-star Hotel Riu Palace Tres Islas three miles from the centre of Corralejo, Fuerteventura costs from £823 to £998 per person, flight inclusive.

Ultimate Holidays (0279 755527)
Destinations include Los Cristianos and Playa de las Americas on the island of Tenerife and Playa Blanca, Puerto del Carmen and Playa de los Pocillos on the island of Lanzarote. For example, a two-week half-board package to the Hotel Princesa Dacil in Los Cristianos costs from £379 to £495 per person, flight inclusive. A two-week half-board package to the Hotel Le Geria in Playa de los Pocillos costs from £565 to £775 per person, including return air fare from London.

Cantabria/Asturias

Brittany Ferries (0705 827701)
Small, family-budget hotels scattered around the countryside and the coast. Bed and breakfast accommodation for seven nights costs from £186 to £223 per person, including return ferry crossings with car and cabin accommodation. One week on a bed and breakfast basis in three- and four-star hotels whilst touring the Picos de Europa, for example, costs from £221 to £366 per person, ferry inclusive.

Casas Cantabricas (0223 328721)
A ferry-inclusive fortnight for a family of four at the Pension La Busta (full board) costs from approximately £385 to £480 per person.

Magic of Spain (081-748 7575)
Hotels ranging from two- to five-star in the mountains and on the beaches. Prices range from £435 to £2000 per person for two weeks, including flights from London.

Secret Spain (0449 737664)
Eastern Asturias. Small mountain or coastal hotels. For example, a seven-night half-board, ferry-inclusive package for a couple with a car at the Hotel Camango, near Ribadesella ranges from £261 to £373 per person.

Travellers' Way (0527 836791)
Asturias. Bed and breakfast accommodation at the Hotel La Torre, near Llanes costs from £25 to £32 per person, per night.

Castile and Leon

Magic of Spain (081-748 7575)
Destinations include Madrid, Toledo and Segovia. Prices range from £435 to £2000 per person for two weeks, including flights from London.

Catalonia

Magic of Spain (081-748 7575)
Destinations include Barcelona, Sitges, Costa Brava and the Pyrenees. Hotels range from two- to five-star. Prices range

from £435 to £2000 per person for two weeks, including flights from London.

PCI Holidays (0444 440606)
Hotels on the coast and in Catalonia's capital Barcelona. For example, two nights' bed and breakfast in the three-star Wilson Hotel in Barcelona costs £128 for two people. This price does not include travel.

Spanish Harbour Holidays (0272 373759)
All family-run establishments, from the simplicity of the two-star Hotel Casamar with twelve bedrooms overlooking the beach at Llafranch to the luxury of the prize-winning Hotel Aigua Blava. Prices for one week's half board, including flights to Barcelona, range from £320 to £765 per person.

Galicia

Brittany Ferries (0705 827701)
One week of luxury bed and breakfast accommodation at Los Reyes Catolicos in Santiago de Compostela starts from £516 to £635 per person, including ferry crossings with car and cabin accommodation.

Secret Spain (0449 737664)
Bed and breakfast in manor houses or hotels near the coast. For example, a seven-night bed and breakfast ferry-inclusive package near Santiago de Compostela costs from £310 to £387 per person.

Travellers' Way (0527 836791)
San Vincente. Bed and breakfast accommodation at the Hotel Mirador Cons de Garda costs from £20 to £25 per night, per person.

Murcia

Connexions (0444 417299)
Hotel and hotel apartments are featured at the La Manga Club which is situated near the city of Murcia. The Club is owned by P&O and is managed by Hyatt Hotels. It extends over 1400 acres of countryside and is made up of three Andalucian-style

villages. For example, seven nights at the five-star Prince Felipe Hotel costs from £614 to £670 per person, based on two sharing. The price includes return air travel. There is a 50 per cent room reduction for two children sharing a second room.

Valencia

Brittany Ferries (0705 827701)
Costa del Azahar: two weeks' bed and breakfast at the Parador in Benicarlo costs from £561 to £761 per person, including ferry crossing with car and cabin accommodation.

Magic of Spain (081-748 7575)
Costa Blanca. From two- to five-star hotels. Prices range from £435 to £2000 per person for two weeks, including flights from London.

Portland Holidays (071-388 5111)
Costa Blanca. A seven-night, full-board package at the Hotel Regente in Benidorm costs from £199 to £250 per person, flight inclusive.

6

SPECIAL INTEREST HOLIDAYS

Spain has rapidly become a special interest holiday destination par excellence. It is a perfect place for a whole range of sporting activities from abseiling to windsurfing – it has every sort of landscape and seascape to match your sporting requirements. And if you want to develop your mind rather than your body, then there are plenty of places in Spain offering courses and special teaching that can help you with this as well.

Below we list a selection of operators who offer activity and special interest holidays: everything from fishing in the Picos de Europa to horse-riding in the Sierra Nevada.

ADVENTURE HOLIDAYS

Exodus (081-675 5550)
Two itineraries in Andalucia: Moorish Andalucia and a Week in Andalucia. For example, the fifteen-day Moorish Andalucia trip explores the cities of Moorish Spain visiting the hill towns and pueblos blancos, walking and riding in the mountains and the secluded National Park of Cazorla. This trip costs from £520 to £590 per person, flight inclusive.

Tall Stories (0932 252002)
Three to six sports in one week on the Catalan coast. Although this is primarily an adults' holiday the company runs one or two specific family weeks. For example, a three-sport week costs from £319 to £369 per person staying on a half-board basis. This price does not include travel.

ANGLING

Anglers World Holidays (0246 221717)
Catalonia. Seven nights' self-catering at an aparthotel in San

Carlos de la Rapita costs from £224 per person, air inclusive. Licences are required by all adult anglers and cost approximately £6 for three weeks. They can be obtained in advance, you will be sent an application form with your booking confirmation.

Secret Spain (0449 737664)
Picos de Europa/Asturias. Staying in a mountain hotel/fishing lodge – including salmon licence. A seven-night, half-board, ferry-inclusive package costs from £345 to £495 per person.

ARCHAEOLOGY

The Travel Club of Upminster (0708 225000)
Discover Minorcan talayots and taulas for one week from £444 per person, including bed and breakfast accommodation, flights and three field trips.

ART HISTORY TOURS

Martin Randall Travel (081-742 3355)
Guided tours mostly in Spring and Autumn. Tours include Madrid and Toledo (6 days – £760), Art in Madrid (4 days – £495), The Road to Santiago (13 days – £1650), Granada and Cordoba (6 days – £785), Andalucia (13 days – £1430), Castile (8 days – £930) and The Pyrenees (10 days – £1350).

Prospect Music & Art Tours (081-995 2151)
Fully-guided tours and cultural weekends. For example, a three-night stay in Barcelona at the four-star Hotel Rivoli Ramblas, with the themes of Gaudi architecture and Miro costs from £395 per person, including scheduled flights. A fully-guided tour of Andalucia for seven nights costs from £895 per person, flight inclusive.

Swan Hellenic (071-831 1515)
A choice of thirteen- and fifteen-day tours of Spain by air and coach. For example, a thirteen-day trip to the Pilgrim's Road to Santiago de Compostela costs £1875 per person. The tour price includes all travel, accommodation and the majority of meals.

The tour is led by an expert and accompanied by a specialist guest lecturer.

BIRDWATCHING

Birding (0797 223223)

The Spanish Steppes. A week-long exploration of the plains and sierras of Extremadura in search of great bustard, black vulture, black stork, imperial eagle, black-shouldered kite and other special birds of Iberia. This tour is in its eighth year of continuous operation. The tour takes place in late May and costs £839 per person, including flights, accommodation, all meals including picnic lunches and the services of the leaders.

The Travel Club of Upminster (0708 225000)

One-week trips to Majorca and Minorca, accompanied by local experts cost from £378 to £428 per person, including flights, transfers and half-board accommodation.

CAMPING

Caravan & Camping Service (071-792 1944)

Campsite reservations service on the Costa Brava, Asturias and the Costa Cantabrica. A return ferry crossing to Dieppe plus one overnight stop in France in both directions and campsite fees for fourteen nights costs from £303. A return ferry crossing to Santander with cabin accommodation and campsite fees for fourteen nights costs up to £1160. The prices quoted are for a family of two adults and two children under fourteen years of age.

Eurocamp Travel (0565 626262)

Catalonia and the Costa Verde. For example, fourteen nights' tent accommodation for two adults and two children, plus car costs from £199 to £825. This price includes short sea ferry crossings.

Eurosites (0706 830888)

Tent and mobile-home holidays on the Costa Brava. For example, two weeks at the Castell Mar site at Badia de Rosas near Figueras costs from £99 to £599. This price is for a party of up to six people inclusive of accommodation and ferry.

Haven Europe (0705 466111)
Catalan Spain – Pals and Torroella de Montgri. For example, a fourteen-night holiday at Pals which was recently voted one of the top twenty-two European camp sites, costs from £199 to £788 for two adults – children under fourteen go free. The price includes a short sea ferry crossing.

Sunsites (0565 625555)
Catalonia (Costa Brava) – Playa de Pals. Twelve nights' tent accommodation at Camping Cypsela costs from £246 to £712 for a party of two adults and up to four children (under fourteen years), including return short sea ferry crossing.

CARAVANS AND MOBILE HOMES

Caravan & Camping Service (071-792 1944)
Campsite reservation service. Locations include the Costa Brava, Asturias and Cantabrias. Ferry-inclusive packages with one overnight stop in France cost from £325. Ferry-inclusive packages to Santander cost up to £1295. These prices include return ferry crossings for car, caravan, two adults and two children under fourteen and campsite fees for fourteen nights.

Sunsites (0565 625555)
Catalonia (Costa Brava) – Playa de Pals. Twelve nights' mobile-home accommodation at Camping Cypsela costs from £390 to £1062 for a party of two adults and up to four children (under fourteen years), including return short sea ferry crossing.

CITY BREAKS

Aeroscope (0608 50103)
Short breaks to cities all over Spain. For example, a two-night trip to Bilbao costs from around £168 to £305 per person, flight inclusive.

A T Mays City Breaks (041 331 1121)
Barcelona and Madrid. For example, a three-night stay at the three-star Hotel Convencion in Madrid costs from £159 to £408 per person, flight inclusive with bed and breakfast accommodation.

Inghams (081-780 0909)

City centre hotels in Barcelona, Madrid and Seville. For example, two nights in Barcelona on a bed and breakfast basis costs from £196 to £239 per person, flight inclusive.

Kirker Holidays (071-231 3333)

Madrid, Barcelona, Seville, Granada and Cordoba. All grades of hotel in central city locations. Weekend breaks start from £236 per person, including scheduled flights, private arrival transfers and accommodation with breakfast. Extra nights cost from £27 per person.

Made to Measure (0243 533333)

Barcelona. Breaks of two to seven days staying at either the five-star Hotel Ritz or the four-star Hotel Colon. Prices on request.

Mundi Color Holidays (071-828 6021)

Breaks are featured to Granada, Cordoba, Seville, Barcelona, Madrid, Santiago, Oviedo, Malaga, Zaragoza, Valencia and Alicante. A sample price of a three-day break to Seville is £235 to £281 per person, based on two nights' bed and breakfast accommodation at a three-star hotel, including flights and transfers.

Thomson Holidays (021 632 6282)

Short breaks from two to seven nights. For example, three nights' bed and breakfast accommodation in Madrid at the Hotel Asturias costs from £219 to £285 per person.

Travellers' Way (0527 836791)

A selection of small privately run hotels throughout Spain which can be booked for stays of any duration from one night to a week or more. For example, one night's stay in Zamora at the Hosteria Real de Zamora costs £28 per person, per night. This price does not include travel.

Ultimate Holidays (0279 755527)

Madrid. For example, a three-night break at the four-star Hotel Agumar costs from £205 to £284 per person, based on two sharing. Prices include air travel.

CLUB HOLIDAYS

Club Med (071-581 1161)
Fully inclusive village holidays in Marbella, Majorca, Ibiza and Cadaques on the Costa Brava. Activities such as snorkelling, tennis, scuba diving, archery, golf and children's clubs are provided. All accommodation is in twin-bedded rooms. One week in Cadaques costs from £439 per person, flight inclusive.

COACH HOLIDAYS

Angela Holidays (0703 403866)
The Costa Brava, Cantabria and an eleven-day tour of southern Spain. For example, the seven-day tour of Cantabria costs from £219 to £289 per person. This price includes return ferry crossings to Bilbao, coach travel, a local guide and three nights' half-board accommodation.

Cosmosair (061-480 5799)
Air-coach holidays to Andalucia. For example, an eight-day trip to Romantic Andalucia, visiting Malaga, Gibraltar, Seville, Granada, Torremolinos, Marbella and Montilla costs from £338 per person, flight inclusive.

Fourwinds Holidays (0452 527656)
An eight-day tour of hidden Spain – the cities of Avila, Salamanca and Toledo costs from £489 per person. This price includes return air fare to Madrid.

Insight Holidays (0800 393 393)
Escorted touring holidays. There are two itineraries to Spain: Highlights of Spain which visits Madrid, Jalon Gorge, Barcelona, Valencia, Alicante, Granada, Seville and Cordoba; and the Best of Spain and Portugal which includes Madrid, Barcelona, Alicante, Granada, Seville, Lisbon, Fatima, Salamanca and Toledo. The Highlights of Spain trip lasts for ten days and costs around £565 per person. The Best of Spain and Portugal tour lasts for fifteen days and costs between £795 and £835 per person.

Mundi Color Holidays (071-828 6021)

Three featured coach tours which include half-board accommodation at four-star hotels and comprehensive guided tours are: a seven-day Wonders of Andalucia; an eight-day Colourful Andalucia and a ten-day The Pilgrims' Way to Santiago. The Wonders of Andalucia holiday costs from £596 to £659 and includes return flights.

COOKING HOLIDAYS

Page & Moy (0533 524433)

Seven-day Spanish cookery courses in Galicia attending cookery demonstrations at the Restaurant El Crisol which featured in 'Floyd on Spain' and 'Spain on a Plate'. Prices range from £429 to £479 per person, flight inclusive. The price includes two nights' half-board and four nights' bed and breakfast accommodation.

CRUISES

Swan Hellenic (071-831 1515)

Cultural cruises in the Mediterranean which have ports of call in Spain. Lectures on a wide range of topics are given on board. The Mediterranean Conquests cruise which visits Italy, France and Spain costs £1595 per person.

CYCLING HOLIDAYS

Bike Tours (0225 480130)

Mountain-bike holidays in the Pyrenees. For example, seven nights' half board, with five days' cycling, four-wheel drive support vehicle and qualified instructor/guide costs £459 per person. A two-week tour in September from Bordeaux to Barcelona costs £489 per person, including thirteen nights' camping, breakfast, afternoon tea, six evening meals, mechanic, nurse, baggage carrying, pick-up service, route notes and maps.

Vélo Vacances (0267 221182)

Traditional tours staying in hotels on a half-board basis; activity tours; off-road tours and camping tours. For example, the ten-day off-road tour in Navarra costs £595 per person, flight inclusive. The accommodation is on a half-board basis.

FLY/DRIVE

Mundi Color Holidays (071-828 6021)

Can be tailormade, but you can also take advantage of suggested itineraries such as The Pilgrims' Way to Santiago, Travel through Asturias, Pueblos Blancos, Cantabria – Picos de Europa, Asturias and Galicia or Catalonia – Pyrenees and Costa Brava. A twelve-day Moorish Splendour holiday through Andalucia costs from £589 to £698 per person. The price includes return flights, bed and breakfast accommodation in three-star hotels and car hire.

GOLFING HOLIDAYS

Above all other sporting activities, Spain in general – and the Costa del Sol in particular – has been the place to go to play golf. In the Eighties golf courses were hard to get on and prices were high. More courses have since been built and Spanish clubs have started to chase business from the casual visitor.

Among the deals on offer to the prospective player are: low green fees and packages with local hotels with items such as one-week hotel stays with free breakfast, free green fees or free tennis. Sometimes not all fees are waived; instead, some may be reduced and shuttle service to the courses provided.

Below is a brief list of some of the Costa del Sol clubs which welcome visitors (green fees can be as little as £20):

Anoreta Gold, Anda del Golf, s/n, Rincon de la Victoria, 2973 Malaga; (95) 240 40 00, or fax (95) 240 40 50: Designed by Jose Maria Canizares, opened in June 1990.

Monte Mayor Golf Club, Urbanization. Los Naranjos Country Club, 29660 N.A. Marbella; (5) 280 08 05 or 281 48 58, or fax (5) 281 48 54: Designed by Pepe Grancedo and opened in 1993.

Golf Club and Hotel El Paraiso, Caretera. Cadiz (km 167), 29680 Estepona, Marbella; (5) 288 30 00 or 288 43 17, or fax (5) 288 20 19.

Atalaya Park Golf Hotel and Resort (located halfway between Estepona and Marbella), ctra. de Cadiz (km168.5), Estepona-Marbella 29688, Malaga; (5) 288 48 01, (5) 288 57 35
Guadalhorce Club de Golf, Ctra. Campanillas, Campanillas, Malaga; (5) 224-36-82: Opened in 1988 and designed by golf architect Kosti Kuronen.

3D Golf plc (0292 263331)
Costa del Sol and Almeria. Self-catering and hotel packages are featured. For example, seven nights in an apartment on the Costa del Sol costs £299 per person from November to June. This price includes flights from Gatwick, car hire between four people and a two-bedroom apartment. It also includes four rounds of pre-booked golf. One week in a hotel on a bed and breakfast basis costs £399 per person.

Longshot Golf Holidays (0730 268621)
Destinations include the Costa del Sol, Valencia, Murcia and Gran Canaria. For example, seven nights' holiday at the five-star Hotel Sidi Sadler, overlooking the El Saler beach costs from £459 to £579 per person, excluding golf fees. The price includes bed and breakfast accommodation, return flights and car hire.

Longwood Holidays (081-551 4494)
Marbella. A seven-night holiday at the Los Monteros Hotel with its own 18-hole golf course costs from £543 to £624 per person, based on two people sharing. The price includes bed and breakfast accommodation, return air fare to Malaga and unlimited golf.

PCI Holidays (0444 440606)
Golfing breaks in Catalonia. Using Pals as a base for a self-catering holiday there is easy access to six or more Championship courses. A two-bedroom apartment within 10 minutes' walk of Pals Golf Club costs from £325 to £601 per week. This price does not include travel.

The Travel Club of Upminster (0708 225000)
One week's golfing holiday in Majorca costs from £588 per person, including green fees and tuition. There is a reduction for accompanying non-golfers. A self-catering option is offered for £260 per person.

HORSERIDING

Aventura (010 34 58 785253)
Accompanied riding holidays are offered in the Sierra Nevada and Alpujarras region. Seven nights cost from £425 to £595 per person, including full board, hire of horse and equipment, guide and transfers to and from Malaga Airport. Air travel is not included.

Secret Spain (0449 737664)
Picos de Europa, northern Spain. Accompanied treks with lunchtime picnics and hotel accommodation. A seven-night, full-board, ferry-inclusive package based on two people travelling with a car and cabin accommodation on the ferry, costs from £770 to £850 per person.

LANGUAGE LEARNING

Euro Academy (081-686 2363)
The courses run all year, are for all ages and are at all levels. Locations include Salamanca, Madrid, Malaga, Nerja and Seville. For example, an intensive course lasting two or three weeks costs from £495 per person, including half-board accommodation and tuition. One to one courses are offered in Malaga, Madrid, Valencia and Seville. Prices are from £480 for tuition plus half-board accommodation.

MUSIC HOLIDAYS

Prospect Music & Art Tours (081-995 2151)
Opera holidays to Barcelona for three nights cost from £425 per person, flight inclusive.

NATURAL HISTORY

Discover the World (06977 48361)
Escorted wildlife breaks in Coto Donana National Park in Andalucia. A four-night package costs £436 per person, including full-board guesthouse accommodation, scheduled

flights, daily excursions and the services of a guide throughout. 'During the weekend we hope to see wild boar, Egyptian mongoose, red deer, fallow deer, spur-thighed tortoise, swallowtail butterfly, greater flamingo, black-winged stilt, great spotted cuckoo, azure-winged magpie, bee-eater, hoopoe, red kite, Spanish Imperial eagle, peregrine falcon, griffon vulture, Egyptian vulture, marsh harrier, Montagu's harrier and many other exciting species.'

Spantrek (0457 836250)
Wildlife holidays in the Picos de Europa, the Pyrenees and Tenerife. For example, fifteen-day all-inclusive packages to the Picos de Europa cost from around £945 per person.

The Travel Club of Upminster (0708 225000)
Nature trailing in Majorca from £344 per person, including half-board accommodation, flights and all accompanied walks.

PAINTING AND DRAWING HOLIDAYS

Artscape Painting Holidays (0702 435990)
Five-day courses in Seville costing £575 per person. This price includes half-board accommodation, return flights and tuition.

PARADORS

Brittany Ferries (0705 827701)
Hotels throughout Spain. For example, a seven-night bed and breakfast stay in Zamora in a restored palace with a swimming pool costs from £355 to £474 per person, based on two sharing. Prices include ferry with car and inside cabin accommodation.

Corona Holidays of London (081-530 2500)
Canary Islands. Parador accommodation is offered on the islands of La Gomera and El Hierro. For example, a stay at the Parador Conde de la Gomera on the island of La Gomera costs from £44.95 to £46.25 per person, per night, based on two people sharing.

Mundi Color Holidays (071-828 6021)
Over seventy Paradors throughout Spain, including the Canary Islands. Individual itineraries and prices are available on request from the Tailor-made department.

Travellers' Way (0527 836791)
Eighty-six Paradors throughout Spain ranging in price from £38 to £78 per person per night. 'Go as you please vouchers' are offered. With these vouchers it is not necessary to make a reservation in advance but availability of accommodation on arrival without prior reservation cannot be guaranteed.

Unicorn Holidays (0582 83 4400)
Individually planned holidays. For example, a fourteen-night fly-drive holiday costs from £1054 to £1378 per person, including scheduled flights from London, car hire, bed and breakfast accommodation, maps and Michelin Green Guide.

PERSONAL DEVELOPMENT

Holidays for Health (071-359 6690)
Holistic workshops covering subjects such as the Alexander technique, T'ai Chi, yoga and reflexology. For example, a week's holiday in October incorporating a massage workshop costs £475 per person, including flights and accommodation.

SAILING

Minorca Sailing Holidays (081-948 2106)
Dinghy and windsurfing tuition at an RYA recognized sailing centre in Ses Salinas. One week's holiday costs from £397 to £663 per person, including accommodation, full use of dinghies and windsurfers, unlimited tuition by qualified RYA instructors and return air travel to Minorca.

TRAIN HOLIDAYS

Excalibur (0202 701123)
'The Andalucian Express, with the elegance of its authentic

1920s rail cars, provides a cruise by rail through the region of Andalucia. Your journey starts in the city of Seville and then moves on to visit the mosque at Cordoba and the Alhambra in Granada. From Granada you will journey on to Ronda and the sherry centre of Jerez before returning to Seville.' Prices on application.

Mundi Color Holidays (071-828 6021)

The Al Andalus Express. Seven-day holidays from Madrid through Andalucia's cities aboard the luxury vintage train. Prices start from £1738 per person and include return flights to Madrid and one night's accommodation at the four-star Palace Hotel in Madrid at each end of the train journey.

WALKING AND TREKKING

Abercrombie & Kent (071-730 9600)

A short walk in the Sierras of Andalucia. The holidays take place during Spring/Summer and Autumn and last for eight days. 'We normally walk in the mornings up to lunchtime and sometimes in the afternoons and evenings mainly along paths and tracks, occasionally steep and rough but never involving scrambling. It should be borne in mind, however, that when travelling we walk for two to five hours a day and therefore a reasonable degree of fitness is required. The holiday is not suitable for young children.' The tour price per person is £940 which includes flights, accommodation, all meals, wine with meals and all other drinks, guided excursions and hosts throughout.

Alternative Travel Group (0865 310399)

Walks along the Pilgrims' Way to Santiago, the Sierras of Catalonia and through the white villages of Andalucia. An eleven-day trip to Catalonia with six days of walking, plus three optional days costs £945 per person, including full-board accommodation. Air travel costs an additional £191 per person.

Explore Worldwide (0252 319448)

Trips range from eight to fifteen days and the average group size is sixteen people. Holidays to Spain include a fifteen-day cultural and adventure tour of Moorish Andalucia with easy day hikes, exploring the cities of Cordoba, Granada and Seville as well as making day walks in the wild mountain landscapes near Cazorla and Ronda; a moderate trek in the foothills of the Sierra Nevada for fifteen days and a moderate to difficult trek in the Picos de Europa for eight days, involving three days light backpacking in the rugged region of Asturias – a delightful, undiscovered part of Spain, with dramatic mountains, flower-filled meadows and picturesque hamlets. Prices range from £490 to £590 per person for the fifteen-day trips and £398 to £449 per person for the eight-day trip. Prices include flights, bed and breakfast accommodation, transport and services of a tour leader.

HF Holidays (081-905 9558)
Calpe, Puerto de la Cruz, Puerto de Soller and Barcelona. For example, in Puerto de Soller, Majorca, leisurely guided walks of five to ten miles are offered – some gentle coastal walks, others ascending up to 2000 feet. Seven- and fourteen-night packages from £391 to £649, including half-board accommodation, walking programme and return scheduled air travel and transfers.

Ramblers Holidays (0707 331133)
One- and two-week rambles which can also combine language improvement and natural history. For example, a one-week trip to Puerto de Andraitx, Majorca costs from £318 to £354 per person. This price includes full-board hotel accommodation and return flights.

Secret Spain (0449 737664)
Picos de Europa/Asturias. Staying in a comfortable hotel near Llanes – marked walks each day with picnic lunches. A seven-night, ferry-inclusive, full-board package costs from £330 to £475 per person.

Sherpa Expeditions (081-577 2717)
Destinations include the Picos de Europa, the Alpujarras, the Sierra Nevada and the Sierra de Tramontana in Majorca. A two-week holiday in the Sierra Nevada costs around £589 per person, including bed and breakfast accommodation in small inns, guides and return air travel.

Spantrek (0457 836250)

Fifteen-day all-inclusive packages to the Picos de Europa from £765 per person. 'Our groups are small (maximum fourteen people), which allows us to cater for a range of ages, needs and abilities. Two leaders, equipped with vehicles are available each day, so we can provide a flexible itinerary.'

Waymark Holidays (0753 516477)

Destinations include the Pyrenees, Galicia, Andalucia and the Picos de Europa. The hotels used range from one to three-star. For example, a seven-night holiday to Alpujarras staying in a three-star hotel on half board costs £350 per person, flight inclusive.

WINDSURFING

Minorca Sailing Holidays (081-948 2106)

Dinghy and windsurfing tuition at RYA recognized sailing centre in Ses Salinas. One week costs from £397 to £663 per person, including accommodation, full use of dinghies and windsurfers, unlimited tuition by qualified RYA instructors and return air travel to Minorca.

WINE TOURS

Arblaster & Clarke Wine Tours (0730 266883)

Destinations include Rioja and northern Spain, Barcelona, Seville and Jerez. For example, a five-day trip to Seville and Jerez costs from £600 to £700. This includes tastings and flights. A six-day trip to Rioja and northern Spain, staying in a parador-style, converted monastery, with tastings and visits to seven leading Bodegas in Rioja and Ribera del Duero/Toro costs £699 per person.

7

HOLIDAY SPAIN

In Britain we are now increasingly familiar with the concept of the Spanish *tapas* bar where customers have a variety of tempting dishes to choose from – all spread out for their delectation.

The travel map of Spain is, in its own way, a mouth-watering sort of *tapas* bar. For the prospective traveller, it is hard to know where to start. Stunning modern architecture? Take a bite from a tasty piece of Barcelona. Glorious history? Try a morsel of Granada, Cordoba or Santiago de Compostela. Just to run through the 'menu' of good places on offer in the entire length and breadth of Spain mightily whets the appetite.

For a family, each of the regions summarized below has something to offer. (Let me state categorically that there is nowhere in Spain where you could not have a rattling good break.)

However, the one factor you may want to consider is the heat: most of Spain is considerably warmer than the UK – but in summer parts can be exceedingly hot.

On one family holiday to a villa in Moraira, north of Benidorm, in July we found the heat excruciating. Even at nighttime there was little obvious falling-off in temperature (at three o'clock in the morning we would study the thermometer and watch astounded as it revealed that it was still over 90 degrees!). Electric fans did nothing more than rearrange the baking air, the only way to cool off was to sit in the swimming pool (not something you really want to do at three o'clock in the morning).

If your children are likely to wilt in the heat, you could consider heading for the northern coast of Spain where you can expect cooling breezes from the Atlantic. In my experience the Balearic and Canary Islands are also less likely to be oppressively hot, thanks to off-shore winds.

Andalucia, particularly inland Andalucia can be ferociously hot, not surprisingly the region is called the frying pan of Spain.

Step out in the post-midday sun and you discover what it must be like to be a rasher of bacon sizzling at Gas Mark Nine.

Touring holidays of Spain need particularly careful planning. For every destination, the guidebooks will show you a crop of 'must see' sights. It is tempting to do your travelling in a trainspotterish way, anxious to 'tick off' as many destinations as you can: sightseeing fatigue and disillusion will rapidly set in (if you have children in tow, they will no doubt make their feelings plain on this at a fairly early stage). Set yourself realistic targets: decide on the sights you really want to see (choose just a handful), concentrate on these – and then anything else you decide to include in your visit will be a bonus.

Before finally choosing a region of Spain for your holiday, spend a little time weighing up the options. I have tried to provide a brief taster of each area: if your appetite is whetted, it's worth undertaking more research by studying one of the many detailed guidebooks.

GALICIA

For those who know Spain very well, Galicia is often the region they guard as their own special secret, the place they would rather keep to themselves secure from the package-tour hordes. Indeed, Galicia is such a wonderful area that it does inspire feelings of protection.

This is Celtic Spain. Judging by their occupation of Brittany, Cornwall, Ireland, Wales and Scotland, the Celts seem to have had a fondness for craggy coastlines. Galicia is no exception. The jagged fjord-like bays cut in and out so frequently and so deeply that the coastline of Galicia stretches for an astonishing 1900 miles around Spain's north-west corner.

And you don't have to look far for another Celtic connection. This is bagpipe country: all fiestas are performed to the sound of the bagpipes' mesmeric chanting.

Galicia's star tourist attraction – in fact, its only well-known attraction – is the city of Santiago de Compostela which has been an important place of pilgrimage since the Middle Ages (for this reason it can claim to be one of the world's first major tourist attractions).

According to legend the Apostle St James – 'Santiago' in Spanish – came to Spain to convert the country to Christianity.

It is said that he preached in the country for seven years before returning to Judaea where he was martyred by Herod. His disciples, forced to leave the country, brought St James's body to Spain and buried it near the spot where their ship landed (supposedly Padron).

The location of the tomb was forgotten for hundreds of years. However, in 813 a star revealed its location to Theodomir, Bishop of Ira Flavia in 813 ('Compostela', from the Latin, means literally 'field of a star'). Like all the best legends, there is a lot of fancy in this and little fact: the best evidence suggests that St James never came within a thousand miles of Spain.

Whatever the facts, during the Middle Ages (when Jerusalem was inaccessible due to the Crusades and Rome was dangerous to visit because of robbers and brigands that preyed on travellers), Santiago grew in stature, attracting at its peak up to two million visitors a year.

Today pilgrims still travel down the Pilgrims' Way to Santiago (El Camino de Santiago): genuine pilgrims travel by foot. But the way across northern Spain is also followed by cyclists and people on horseback (and doubtless any other form of locomotion).

Waiting for them is one of the most attractive cities in Spain. Santiago cathedral is certainly one of the finest buildings in the world. Outside the cathedral, the Plaza de Espana is a magnificent square, flanked on one side by the Hotel Los Reyes Catolicos, a Parador hotel housed in the Royal Pilgrims' Hostel built in the sixteenth century in the grand style. A stay here is a guaranteed highlight of any visit to Galicia.

My favourite part of Galicia is the south-west corner of the region, next to the Portuguese border. Bayona is a glorious spot but on the face of things a generally unremarkable seaside place set on a superb bay. It does have an outstanding Parador and an extraordinary history (it was the first place in the Old World to learn of the discovery of the New World when the Pinta arrived here in 1493 with astonishing news of Columbus's voyage to the Americas).

South of Bayona is the busy frontier town of Tuy (with a parador) and beyond the border lies northern Portugal, the happiest of hunting grounds for the independent traveller (Ponte de Lima is a particular treasure, but it would be hard work to find a dud place here).

Further up the coast from Bayona you can choose from a selection of delightful seaside places. Cambados has its impressive traditional manor houses; La Toja is a sophisticated resort with a choice of excellent hotels; and Pontevedra, which boasts a fine Parador and selection of lovely old buildings. The main town in the area is Vigo, a long-established port from which ships sailed to and from Spain's American colonies, returning laden with gold.

Inland lie several attractive old towns set in magnificent countryside. The best of these is Lugo, still circled by its impressive Roman walls.

On the north coast of Galicia the chief port is La Coruna, known to the English as Corunna and famous as the burial place of Sir John Moore, a distinguished soldier who died in the Napoleonic wars and whose death was celebrated in a poem by Charles Wolfe ("Not a drum was heard, nor a funeral note...").

La Coruna is also famous for its glazed balconies (they are particularly good on the Avenida de la Marina). Surprisingly there is no Parador in La Coruna, but more surprisingly there is one in nearby Ferrol, an ugly naval town whose principal claim to fame is that it was the birthplace of General Franco.

One of my favourite Paradors is in the small town of Villalba, a short drive inland from La Coruna. The hotel is housed in an extraordinary octagonal fortress, complete with drawbridge, and has just half a dozen bedrooms (albeit massive rooms complete with stout walls and slit windows). A night here is a genuine treat.

'GREEN' SPAIN: CANTABRIA AND ASTURIAS

Driving through Asturias, I will never forget the shock at seeing a dead bear lying at the side of the road. Dead dogs and dead cats are regrettable though unsurprising – but a dead bear? Indeed wild bears – and wolves – still inhabit the wild countryside of the Picos de Europa (an obvious lack of road sense not withstanding).

It was the very wildness of this countryside which proved such an insurmountable barrier to the invading Moors. Asturias was the one part of Spain they failed to conquer. The defeat of the Moors at Covadonga in 722, a short drive from Cangas de Onis, marked the start of the La Reconquista – a 770-year struggle to throw the Moors out of Spain.

Most visitors to Cangas de Onis are drawn not by its history but because it provides a good base for exploring the extraordinary Picos de Europa mountains, a massive series of peaks, the tallest of which rise to over 2600m (8350ft) and offer some of the best walking country in the whole of Europe. One of the favourite walking trips is to take the cable car at Fuente De (which has a fine Parador). The cable-car ride up the 800m cliffs does the hard work: you can take a more leisurely stroll back to base, looking out for chamois and soaring eagles and vultures.

If you prefer to stick to your car there are plenty of good drives (but take care on the winding roads – some of the drops are terrifying!). The Desfiladero de La Hermida which is along the road between Panes and Potes has been described as the Spanish Grand Canyon.

The main town of Asturias is Oviedo, a city with a fine cathedral and a one-way traffic system of mindboggling complexity. Nearby is the port of Gijon, worth a look for its well-preserved Roman baths and its fine modern Parador.

Cantabria is better known to British travellers through Brittany Ferries service to Santander from Plymouth. Santander is well worth a visit: its port, like all ports, is a bit grim – but it has a lively town centre and an attractive resort called El Sardinero complete with casino and a fine beach.

Cantabria's most notable tourist attraction lies twenty miles away: Santillana del Mar. This handsomely preserved town – all cobbled streets and seigneurial mansions – was described by Jean-Paul Sartre as 'the prettiest village in Spain'. As you might expect, the town has a fine Parador housed in a grand old house.

A short drive away are the caves of Altamira, which rank with Lascaux in France in having some most magnificent cave paintings. Like Lascaux they have had to be closed to the public since visitors' breath was destroying the very things they had come to see. The museum however is well worth a look.

Of Cantabria's seaside places, Laredo is the nearest thing to one of the big beach resorts of the Mediterranean Costas.

BASQUE COUNTRY, NAVARRA AND NORTHERN ARAGON

For those travellers familiar with Spain at its Mediterranean end, the northern fringe of the country can come as a huge surprise. This is green Spain, cool Spain, a land of mountains, a country with its feet planted firmly in the boisterous waters of the Bay of Biscay.

Drive east from Santander towards the French border and you pass through a landscape that might have been copied from Switzerland. Craggy mountain tops; green, green grass; and huge swathes of forest.

And then you bump into the outskirts of Bilbao: steaming factories, smoking stinking chemical plants and rows of neat tower blocks, all of which provide an agreeable reminder of busy industrial Birmingham in the Sixties. You notice the graffiti slogans on walls, bus shelters, roofs, tunnels – even on the very road itself. And everywhere you face misdirection with road signs that have had their Castilian place names messily paint-sprayed out.

With a jolt you realize that now you are in the Basque Country, a region familiar to us not for its lush countryside but for the intermittent news reports of murdered policemen and IRA-style bombings carried out by ETA terrorists. (Happily, greater autonomy for the Basques, public revulsion at the political violence and the arrest of prominent ETA leaders has resulted in a marked scaling-down of terrorist activities.)

The rush to embrace the Basque language – which largely consists of words that look like the very worst hands at Scrabble (all Js, Xs, Zs, Ks and Vs) – poses problems for the newly arrived motorist. Presumably in deference to local sensibilities, sometimes only the Basque name will be shown on a signpost – fine if you know, for example, that Hondarribia is also Fuenterrabia (if you don't know, expect a mighty driver/navigator barney).

A little way east of Bilbao, a motorway exit sign points towards 'Gernika', the Basque name for Guernica, the spiritual capital of the Basque Country. The town achieved an awful celebrity on 27 April 1937 when the German Air Force – which was supporting Franco in the Civil War – used Guernica as a test bed for its theories on saturation bombing.

For three and a quarter hours a squadron of Junkers and Heinkel bombers and Heinkel fighters bombed and strafed the town killing over 1600 people and injuring hundreds more. The terror inflicted on this quiet country town, busy with market-day visitors, was captured in what is perhaps the most famous 20th-century work of art: Picasso's painting 'Guernica'.

The town has been pleasantly rebuilt, leaving no obvious reminders of this awful episode in its history. You can still see the old parliament building, miraculously unscathed by the attack, and within a little Greek temple are the remains of the famous Tree of Guernica beneath which the parliament used to meet.

There is no obvious memorial to the bombing. For the Spanish the hurt caused by the Civil War is probably still too fresh to need further public recollections of the misery. At lunchtime the sunny streets were deserted except for the occasional knot of laughing schoolchildren.

A short drive away lies the Basque Coast, one of the world's most handsome stretches of coastline. The old whaling port of Getaria is a gem. The harbour is still busy with trawlers unloading fish. Well before lunchtime, restaurants have their open-air barbecues at full heat to cook the squid – *chipirones* – for which the town is famous.

Getaria's principal claim to fame however is navigator Juan Sebastian Elcano who sailed with Magellan on his 16th-century circumnavigation of the world. After Magellan was murdered in the Philippines it was left to Elcano to bring the ship home, making him the world's first circumnavigator – a feat celebrated with a memorial built in a bizarre Stalinist epic style at the entrance to town.

After all the surprises so far encountered in just a few hours' drive from the ferry port, you might have thought you were ready for anything. Nothing however can prepare you for the stunning spectacle of San Sebastian. Ideally you should be led blindfold to the lookout point at the top of Monte Igueldo: open your eyes and you will be treated to one of the most sumptuous views in the whole of Spain.

In the foreground is the majestic sweep of La Concha beach, behind the golden sand and Edwardian promenade you can pick out the Miramar Palace, once the summer residence of the Spanish royal family, and way behind the town towards the French border are more of those craggy mountains. Above San

Sebastian, opposite you on Monte Urgull, towers a huge statue of Christ (masked by scaffolding at present). It would be easy to imagine you had been spirited away to Rio de Janeiro and that spread out below was the Copacabana.

You might have thought that places like San Sebastian were now extinct. It is a good old-fashioned seaside resort that manages to be elegant yet without the slightest trace of pretention. For example, a few steps away from the viewpoint at Monte Igueldo is a mini-funfair complete with dodgems and stalls inviting you to shoot a duck or burst a balloon to win a goldfish.

Wander along the prom during the evening *gran paseo* and while there are plenty of chic-looking women in designer outfits, the beach will be full of kids playing kickabout football or families knocking a volley-ball around. You could spend hours wandering up and down the paved walkway.

Ex-Cardiff City and Liverpool player John Toshack, highly revered Welsh manager of local team Real Sociedad, is often to be seen strolling the prom deep in happy contemplation.

Follow the prom to its westernmost point and it leads to the Combs of the Wind, a striking sculpture of iron tentacles by local artist Eduardo Chillida. Watch out for the vents through which mighty blasts of air are blown by the rising and falling sea – come at high tide to enjoy this unusual entertainment at its best.

The city's plushest accommodation is to be found at the Hotel Maria Cristina which has double rooms from £120 per night. This Belle Epoque delight is guarded by a doorman comically overdressed in a uniform straight from a Quality Street tin. It's all extremely smart, but if you enter dressed only in jeans and trainers you will still be treated to a warm salute.

Perhaps San Sebastian's greatest attraction is the old town with its narrow streets bursting with restaurants and *tapas* bars. There are a couple of places where people go to be seen rather than to eat, but for the most part the restaurants are ones local residents go to for a regular evening out. A decent set meal can be had for less than £12 a head at even the smartest place.

Food is taken very seriously here. As well as a Gastronomic Academy, San Sebastian has more than thirty *Sociedades Recreativas*: men-only food clubs where members cook each other meals in well-appointed club kitchens.

San Sebastian is a place to spend a very happy week or two. It is such a pleasant spot, one fears for its future: will success spoil it in the way that it has spoilt similar resorts on the Mediterranean? Best to see it now to be on the safe side.

Take the Jaizkibel Road out of San Sebastian for another luscious dollop of coastline. The road leads to Fuenterrabia which has an impressive old town and an even more impressive Parador hotel in the former Palace of Carlos V. The Parador is currently undergoing refurbishment – and no date has yet been set for its reopening. But while you may not be able to spend the night in the old town, you can wander about and enjoy its magnificently preserved houses with their ornate balconies and carved wood cornices. Caged birds fill the air with merry song.

In the Sixties the frontier between France and Spain used to be a dividing line as marked as the Berlin Wall. On one side was prosperous, thriving, civilized France – on the other was Franco's Spain, a place that exhibited the signs of Third World neglect: a country of peasants and grinding poverty.

Now you can cross the border by car and hardly recognize the transition from one country to another. The new open frontier has thankfully ended the interminable passport control queues. So now within half an hour of sunning yourself in San Sebastian, you can be across the frontier and dipping your toes in the sea at St Jean de Luz on the French side of the Basque coast.

Navarre's most famous place is the city of Pamplona, thanks to its starring role in one of Hemingway's best-known books *Fiesta* (its American title is *The Sun Also Rises*). During its week-long San Fermin festival – with its famous morning running of the bulls – Pamplona attracts hordes of visitors.

It used to attract the sort of showbiz crowd now lured to sporting events like Wimbledon and the Monaco Grand Prix. Nowadays the running of the bulls attracts a huge following among student-age travellers – largely foreigners – who move into the city on 6 July and remain camped there for a week like an army of occupation spreading out over all available grass verges.

In his recent biography *Hemingway: A Life Without Consequences*, James R Mellow reveals that Hemingway was worried that the Pamplona fiesta would be damaged by publicity. Asked to write a travel article about San Fermin, Hemingway declined, saying that providing too much coverage for the fiesta would be a mistake. He thought that a company like Thomas Cook would begin running tours to Pamplona and ruin it.

'Practically all the people that deserved to be at Pamplona were there this year,' he wrote. But shortly afterwards, in 1927, Hemingway produced *Fiesta* whose instant popularity effectively ruined *los sanfermines* much more thoroughly than any travel feature ever could have.

During the festival, Pamplona is particularly popular with Australians and New Zealanders who gather in what they call Mussel Bar Square to hurl themselves off the top of the fountain into, they hope, the waiting arms of their friends (these hopes sometimes prove to be misplaced).

Other places worth looking at include Olite, an unspoiled medieval town which has been impressively well restored; and Sanguesa, on the Rio Aragon, which has a lovely medieval church: Santa Maria la Real.

A short way south-east, in northern Aragon, is the town of Sos del Rey Catolico: birthplace of the Catholic King Ferdinand of Aragon. There is a modern Parador here, built in the late Seventies, but built with traditional materials.

Also worth searching out is Ordesa National Park, little known outside Spain, but a magnificent place with an abundance of wildlife and some spectacular views of the high peaks of the Pyrenees.

Zaragoza is Aragon's capital: it's a big but wholly attractive city with a lively feel. One of its best sights is Primo de Rivera park with an art nouveau masterpiece (Zaragoza is something of an art nouveau treasure house): a wrought-iron bandstand topped with a pineapple dome.

CATALONIA AND BARCELONA

It is not hard to see why the Catalans see themselves as a nation separate from the rest of Spain. Certainly, they have their own language but more than this their brisk way of life stands in stark contrast to slow-paced Andalucia in the south. Catalonia seems to have more in common with, say, France or Italy than the rest of Spain.

The charms of Barcelona are well known (and are covered in detail in 'City Breaks' in Chapter Eight) but even without Barcelona, Catalonia has much to offer the visitor.

Families are most likely to be attracted to the Costa Brava, the coast which runs from the French border down to Blanes. The Costa Brava was the first of the Costas to become familiar to British travellers with resorts like Lloret de Mar and Tossa de Mar becoming synonymous with the modern concept of the package-holiday resort.

Lloret de Mar is the least agreeable of Costa Brava's resorts: a strip of unprepossessing burger bars, bland hotels and too busy roads. For a family beach holiday, the resorts worth considering are Tossa de Mar, Calella de Palafrugell, Aiguablava and Cadaques. Along the coast there are plenty of small coves and quiet beaches which offer good bases such as Tamariu, south of Aiguablava.

The Costa Dorada, south of Barcelona, is generally less developed than the Costa Brava. The best-known resort now is Sitges which has become famous as something of a gay resort. The main package-holiday resort is Salou which has some good beaches but is probably best avoided in the summer peak. Other seaside places worth considering include Tarragona (its magnificent Roman Devil's Bridge is worth a look) and Cambrils, a classier alternative to downmarket Salou.

At the southern end of Catalonia lies the Ebro Delta, the largest wetlands in the region and – second to France's Camargue – the most important aquatic environment in the western Mediterranean. It is famous for growing rice; and even better known for its bird population which includes ducks, coots, egrets and, sometimes, flamingos.

Away from the coast, Catalonia has much to offer the tourist. Apart from the fine countryside of the Pyrenees and the Aigues Tortes national park, there is a fine crop of interesting cities including Lerida, Montserrat, Poblet, Gerona and Figueras.

Figueras should be visited if only for the Teatre-Museu Dali, a permanent exhibition of the extraordinary work of the late surrealist artist Salvador Dali who was born in the town.

OLD CASTILE AND LEON

This is the heart of old Spain, a place of fortresses (the *castillos* that gave Castile its name) from which the war of Reconquista was waged against the Moors.

One of my favourite cities in the area is Leon which boasts a fine Gothic cathedral and an equally fine hotel – the San Marcos – which used to be a hostel and hospital for pilgrims *en route* to Santiago. The cathedral is famous for its stained-glass windows, the equal of Chartres. The guidebooks tell you that the cathedral has 125 windows and 57 oculi producing an area of glass totalling 1200 square metres – in fact, so much glass and so little wall that the cathedral is in danger of collapsing!

You don't have to be a hotel guest to enjoy the San Marcos Monastery, though a night here would be a highlight of the holiday (so think about pushing the boat out). The magnificent 100metre facade of the monastery, done in a style known as platerseque, barely prepares you for its even more astonishing interior. Take a look inside if only to see the touchingly beautiful 11th-century ivory Carrizo Crucifix displayed in the archaeological museum.

Burgos has a couple of claims to fame. Firstly, its huge Gothic cathedral, outranked in size only by those in Seville and Toledo. Burgos's other principal claim to noteworthiness is that it was the birthplace of El Cid (his tomb is in the cathedral). El Cid, whose exploits were celebrated in a Hollywood film, distinguished himself in the war of Reconquest against the Moors.

Lying between Leon and Burgos is Rioja country. The principal centre of wine production is Haro; Rioja bodegas which offer wine tastings, are near the railway station. There is a wine museum in the town which offers an explanation of how Rioja is made (but unfortunately no tastings!).

An old university town, Salamanca has been called the 'Spanish Oxford'. While it may no longer have the pre-eminence of Oxford, it still boasts a large student population (particularly during the summer months when it plays host to large numbers of language students).

Begin your visit in the Plaza Mayor, the centre of life in the city. The main sights include the two intertwined cathedrals: the Catedral Nueva and the Romanesque Catedral Vieja – and the Patio de Las Escuelas, a small square off the Calle Libreros, surrounded by buildings in the plateresque style.

Valladolid is another university city with a rich history: Columbus and the writer Cervantes lived here. At one point in its history, it vied with Madrid as the royal capital. Unfortunately the old part of the city has not been preserved or as carefully maintained as Salamanca. It does however have excellent Holy Week processions. Best of the sights is the 15th-century Colegio de San Gregorio which has one of Spain's finest collections of religious art.

Zamora is not a city that many people are likely to pass through by chance, so it receives far fewer tourists than comparable Spanish cities. A shame for Zamora, good news for the tourist who makes the effort. It has a marvellous cathedral (complete with a Byzantine-inspired dome and 'fish-scale' tiles and the cathedral museum has the impressive 'Black Tapestries'). Also look out for the Holy Week museum with displays from Zamora's Holy Week processions. Have a look – better still book a room – at the Parador Condes de Alba de Aliste in Plaza de Viriato, housed in a 15th-century ducal palace.

Students of history will enjoy a visit to nearby Tordesillas where, under the supervision of Pope Alexander VI, Spain and Portugal divided South America between them. It has a modern Parador uncomfortably near the main road.

MADRID AND SURROUNDING AREA

Madrid and its attractions as a city-break destination are covered in the next chapter. If you are planning a longer stay, Madrid is handily placed for a touring holiday.

Segovia is probably the best known of Madrid's near neighbours thanks to its magnificent Roman aqueduct – some 800 metres long and 30 metres high, and held together without a dot of mortar! Segovia is a ravishingly good-looking place with a fairy-tale castle, the Alcazar, and a cathedral which is all pinnacles and cupolas.

El Escorial, situated on a foothill of the Sierra de Guadarrama to the north-west of Madrid, was an unremarkable village until Philip II chose it as the site for his monastery palace. The building, which was the largest Spanish building of the Renaissance, is now one of Spain's biggest tourist attractions. While El Escorial is certainly an impressive sight, the interior is actually rather ordinary – a quick look–see is probably the order of the day.

Five miles north of El Escorial is the Valle de los Caidos (the Valley of the Fallen), dominated by a huge cross (reckoned to be the largest in Spain). Conceived by General Franco as a memorial to the dead of the Spanish Civil War, it seems that it was intended to serve more as a memorial to Franco.

At 1131 metres Avila is the highest of Spain's provincial capitals and consequently suffers cold winters (even in May you can expect it to be fairly chilly). This attractive town's principal claim to fame is as the birthplace of Saint Teresa of Avila and consequently has a large number of impressive religious buildings.

Former capital of Spain, Toledo is still in every inch a city of great stature. It stands on a rocky bluff, looking hugely impressive behind its ramparts. It is a compact place (refreshing news for the weary sightseer) but there is much to see – and the delight of the place is simply to wander around, discovering things serendipitously. Chief sight (inevitably for a Spanish city) is the cathedral. The other chief attraction is El Greco's 'The Burial of the Count of Orgaz' which can be seen in an annexe to the church of Santo Tome (expect a long queue).

Curiously more people will know Aranjuez as a piece of music (Rodrigo's 'Concierto de Aranjuez') than as a city. Not quite in the Toledo league, it is a charming enough spot – once the spring and autumn retreat of the Spanish monarchs. The Royal Palace is worth a look, along with the Prince's Garden and the fancifully named Labourer's Cottage (a modest palace, actually). Nearby Chinchon is a picturesque spot, best known in Spain for its *anis* distilleries.

EXTREMADURA AND NEW CASTILE

Of all the areas of Spain, this is the one probably most neglected by tourists. For anyone heading south or west of Madrid, the temptation is to race on across this plain – infernally hot during the summer – to the final destination.

This is a shame, because this region may have no great names to attract the tourists, but it has many agreeable and fascinating spots (all the more worth searching out because they are unlikely to be deluged with visiting coachloads of camera-toting grockles).

For lovers of Spanish literature, perhaps the region's chief claim to fame is that this is 'Quixote country', home of Don Quixote – the Man of La Mancha (La Mancha means 'the dry land'). In Spain, La Mancha is probably best known for its Manchego cheese (a staple of *tapas* bars), but most tourists probably come here to follow in the footsteps of the knight errant.

At Consuegra, for example, south-east of Toledo you can see the line of windmills that might have inspired Don Quixote to tilt at them. (Consuegra has a good tourist information centre which can supply you with all the *Ruta de Don Quixote* information you need). At El Toboso, you can visit the 'home' of Dulcinea – Cervantes' slatternly princess – which has been turned into a museum.

The old quarter of Cuenca has an extraordinary setting surrounded on three sides by the deep gorges of the rivers Jucar and Huecar. It is a congested tangle of narrow streets and tall houses (and famous Hanging Houses which overhang the rock face in spectacular fashion). It is a fashionable weekend spot for people from Madrid: hence a fine museum of abstract art and a new Parador, the latest addition to the Parador chain.

As a base for exploring La Mancha, Ciudad Real offers a useful base. It has an interesting Mudejar-style gateway and a 16th-century cathedral.

To the west in Extremadura, Trujillo is a fascinating town with a series of handsome mansions built on the riches of the discoveries in the New World. It is described as 'the nursery of the Conquistadores' as it is said that twenty American nations were conceived here. Its most famous son is Francisco Pizarro, the cruel conqueror of Peru: a swineherd who went on to marry an Inca princess.

Caceres, like Trujillo, has an attractive old town with a number of seigneurial mansions built out of the riches of the New World. The provincial museum has a contemporary art section with works by Miro, Arroyo and Picasso.

Merida was the Roman capital of Lusitania: visitors here can see more Roman remains than in any other city in Spain. As well as temples, the Romans built a theatre, arena and a 400 - metre racecourse – the arena is particularly worth seeing.

MURCIA AND VALENCIA

While this region – known as the Levant – may have more compelling places to visit, there is only one town here whose name is familiar to most northern Europeans. So well known, in fact, that its very name has become synonymous with the modern package holiday: Benidorm.

In many places throughout Benidorm you can see photographs of the way the place used to be. Like pictures which show Neil Kinnock when he was seven years old with a full head of hair, the display of these photos is meant to offer some harmless amusement. Hard to believe, they say, but under this Manhattan skyline of tower block hotels and apartments, there used to be a small seaside village.

Before tourism came, there was real life here. It hasn't always been paella parties and topless sunbathing on the beach. Benidorm's tuna fishermen were famous throughout the Mediterranean for their skill in landing the big catches.

The old photographs prove that until the mid-Fifties Benidorm amounted to nothing more than some houses, a few holiday villas and a handful of hotels. Families in Madrid and nearby Alcoy who could afford a Seat 600 came with their luggage piled on the roofrack for a couple of weeks by the sea.

But in the early Fifties when British companies like Horizon and Skytours were developing the concept of the charter flight and the cheap package holiday, it was inevitable that they would eventually light upon Benidorm. Protected from cold north winds by a barrier of high mountains, and in a choice spot facing south, it had a good winter climate and tremendous potential as a year-round destination (an important consideration for tour operators who needed to keep their expensive fleets of charter aircraft operating during the off-season).

As the Fifties gave way to the Swinging Sixties, more than any other resort Benidorm benefited from the boom in package holidays. The town was built as a Sixties image of urban Britain reflecting our fascination for tower blocks: skyscraping hotels were constructed at a breathtaking rate.

In 1968, when Benidorm was already attracting a million visitors a year, twenty-eight new hotels were opened in one year alone. Now Benidorm receives around four million visitors a year; there are more than 150 hotels – with 36,000 hotel rooms it offers more accommodation than any other town or city in Spain (in terms of hotel capacity it is the third biggest in Europe after London and Paris).

In the peak season during August, Benidorm's population increases to a quarter of a million, over five times its normal size – if you use the beach, you are likely to find yourself sharing it with 185,000 other people.

A quarter of Benidorm's overseas visitors are British – the next biggest foreign market is the Netherlands which accounts for around seven per cent of the total – less than a third of the number of British visitors.

'When anyone thinks of Benidorm, they think of fish and chips,' complains Roc Gregori, the director of Benidorm's Tourist Board. 'Do you know how many fish and chip shops there are in the whole of Benidorm? Two. Out of a thousand bars and restaurants here, there are only 200 English pubs. People have the wrong idea about Benidorm.'

It certainly may not be Juan-les-Pins, but apart from its size and its tower-block scenery it's hard to fault Benidorm. It's kept spotlessly neat, the beaches are among the cleanest in the world – with three EEC Blue Flags for high standards of hygiene and safety. Over £100 million has been spent smartening the resort up – an exercise in civic pride that many other resorts might do well to copy.

Spain's third biggest city, Valencia lacks the instant appeal of its bigger brothers: Barcelona and Madrid. However, there is plenty here to interest the visitor for a couple of days. The labyrinth-like streets of the Barrio del Carmen – the old part of the city – are perfect for idle wandering. Other highlights include the cathedral, a good art museum (works by El Greco, Goya and Velazquez), and one of the biggest fruit and vegetable markets in Europe.

Today most people know Alicante as the gateway airport for Benidorm, but in Classical times the Greeks and Romans were attracted here by its luminous skies (the Romans called it Lucentum – the city of light). Despite the depredations of tourism, it still remains an attractive place, with pleasant esplanades, good beaches and fine terrace cafés.

Murcia may be the commercial centre of the region but it is an agreeable, slow-paced city with a fine cathedral and a sumptuous casino.

ANDALUCIA

This huge region in southern Spain – one-sixth of the whole of the country – is in many ways everyone's idea of Holiday

Spain. Of course, there are the famous resorts like Marbella and Torremolinos, and the famous historical cities like Granada and Seville – but more than that, with its distinctive white villages, its flamenco dancers, its olive groves, its madcap fiestas and its lush greensward golf courses, it summons up the whole glorious image of Spanish holidays.

There are three 'Costas': the Costa de Almeria, the Costa del Sol and the lesser known Costa de la Luz.

Almeria is often described as the dustbowl of Spain. Indeed, inland is a desert that has been a boon to European film-makers. An area called Mini-Hollywood has been surprisingly productive: *Lawrence of Arabia* was filmed here – but its most famous products were the 'spaghetti westerns' including *A Fistful of Dollars.*

The beaches along Almeria are good, particularly on the eastern side. Roquetas de Mar and Aguadulce have been developed but not too unpleasantly. Probably the most appealing of the resorts is El Cabo de Gata. The resort most promoted in the UK is Mojacar. It is newly developed but, surprisingly for new development in Spain, it has been done reasonably sympathetically.

'Sympathetic development' and the 'Costa del Sol' are terms that do not fit together unfortunately. The better part of the Sun Coast is to the east: better not so much in terms of scenery – it's actually rather drab – but because it is rather less built-up. The town of Nerja has its charms, including a Parador and show caves at the Cuevas de Nerja. Other seaside places worth a look include Almunecar and Salobrena.

Malaga is a city that most tourists fly to and then drive out of as fast as possible. Indeed, on the face of things it seems a fairly grim place – but it has its moments (even grudging Michelin affords it a star). There are two good Moorish citadels: the Alcazaba and Gibralfaro – and in the old streets of the town there are plenty of good restaurants, with some particularly fine fish and seafood cafés.

West of Malaga lie the major resorts of the Costa del Sol: Torremolinos, Fuengirola and Marbella. Torremolinos, like Benidorm, may not be everybody's cup of tea but it does its job as a big brash resort to the obvious satisfaction of most visitors. As a lively place offering a lot of activities, it has a lot of advantages as a family holiday destination.

Neighbouring Fuengirola is less developed and less frenetic

than Torremolinos. It has an older clientele, appealing to families who are looking for a quieter time: a place for pedalos and windsurfing.

Despite its well-publicized connection with British criminals on the run, Marbella is very much the up-market resort of the Costa del Sol. The latest up-market addition to the coast is the marina and casino complex of Puerto Banus – not quite the 'Spanish Saint Tropez' claimed in the tourist promotion – but it is well worth visiting just to gaze at the wealthy on board the palatial yachts.

Gibraltar may not be a political part of Spain – much to the continued disgruntlement of Spanish politicians – it inevitably features as an attraction of the Costa del Sol because since 1985 it has been accessible from Spain (Franco closed the border in 1967). Gibraltar merits a visit if only because of the novelty of seeing a small piece of Britain (British bobbies and all) set on the southern tip of the Iberian peninsular.

From the top of the Rock of Gibraltar you can look over the Straits to Africa. From nearby Algeciras you can catch a ferry to Morocco: there are crossings to Tangier every day by ferry and hydrofoil (the hydrofoil takes an hour).

The quiet Costa de la Luz – the Coast of Light – stands in almost complete contrast to the helter skelter life of the Costa del Sol. This Atlantic-facing coast, which runs down from the Portuguese border to Gibraltar, offers attractive (and often windy) beaches and, perhaps best of all, Spain's finest national park.

Thanks to its stiff Atlantic breezes, the resort of Tarifa has become Spain's – and Europe's – top windsurfing place, offering more rental shops and equipment specialists than you could shake an Andalucian stick at. Tarifa Beach, north-west of Tarifa, offers fine stretches of sand and crashing rollers.

Royal hunters used to frequent what is now the Coto Donana National Park, shooting the exotic birds, deer and wild boar that lived there. Happily the wildlife is now protected and the National Park has become one of the best known in Europe. Entry is carefully controlled, restricted to organized tours in summer and winter. Visitors can normally expect to see flamingos, imperial eagles, deer and wild boar.

Cadiz has been a port for more than 3000 years, trading with everybody from the Phoenicians, Carthaginians and Romans through to the Visigoths and Moors. There are no particularly great sights here. Cadiz is worth visiting more for its *louche* charm.

Away from the seaside, inland Andalucia has much to offer. Lovers of sherry will be keen to visit Jerez de la Frontera, home of the blended wine that bears its name ('jerez' proved too much for the English tongue – we altered it to 'sherry'). There are many bodegas offering tours and tastings.

The whitewashed houses of Ronda, a town poised above a precipitous gorge, provide a fine introduction to the charms of rural Andalucia. Ronda is one of the 'pueblos blancos' – white towns – that are so characteristic of the region: others include Castellar de la Frontera, Jimena de la Frontera, Gaucin, Setenil, Olvera and Teba.

Of Andalucia's major tourist places, Seville is pre-eminent (we cover the city in more detail in the following chapter). But judging by the queues outside the main sights, my guess is that Granada attracts more visitors.

'Nothing in life is sadder than to be blind in the Alhambra,' goes an old Arab saying. The words still ring true today. Granada's Alhambra palace is a visual feast – but even Granada itself looks good, framed as it is by the snow-capped Sierra Nevada mountains.

The high spot, literally and metaphorically, is the old Moorish palace of Alhambra. More than just a palace, it is a complex made up of a royal palace (the Casa Real), the gardens of the Generalife, and the Alcazaba fortress. The palace itself is a sumptuous edifice of richly decorated halls and serene patios.

In my opinion Andalucia's greatest treasure is Cordoba. Playing second fiddle to its near neighbour Seville severely injures the fierce pride of the Cordobans. The citizens of Cordoba will tell you of a conspiracy directed against it by the political bosses of the autonomous province of Andalucia. People say that it is because Cordoba has a communist-controlled council that it has been ignored – while Seville has had government riches heaped upon it in plenty.

It is easy to sympathize with Cordoba's plight. In the tenth century, under the control of the Moors, it was one of Europe's great cities – certainly it was the wealthiest. It was a seat of learning, a centre of trade, a place of magnificent buildings and good living: it was an Islamic Versailles.

The extraordinary thing about Cordoba is not that so much of this rich history has vanished (the Christian reconquerors of

Spain had all the charm and discernment of English football supporters when it came to caring for the Moorish heritage) but that such a magnificent abundance remains.

The attractions of Seville's Alcazar and Granada's Alhambra are well known – Cordoba's Mezquita and its Jewish quarter may be less famous but they are in many ways much more magnificent. (Cordoba's sights are all the more splendid precisely because they are so unexpected.)

Cordoba's outskirts suggest that you might be entering Slough rather than approaching a historical marvel – but be patient. Even if it were just for the old Jewish quarter (*La Juderia*) and the surrounding labyrinth of white alleyways leading to exquisite patioed houses, Cordoba would demand your admiration and affection.

The Mezquita however demands open-mouthed astonishment. Stepping inside into its cool shade, nothing quite prepares you for the apparently endless forest of pillars that support the distinctive red-and-white Moorish arches.

A short drive from Cordoba it's worth searching out two neighbouring Andalucian jewels: Baeza and Ubeda. Ubeda is particularly delightful: visit the Plaza Vazquez de Molina with its sublime church of El Salvador and the neighbouring Parador housed in a magnificent 16th-century mansion.

Balearic Islands

The four main Balearic Islands: Majorca, Minorca, Ibiza and Formentera are lumped together as if they were all much the same sort of place. In fact, each is quite different – and it would be a rash guidebook writer who dared to characterize each island in a simple description. For although Majorca has overdeveloped parts, for example, it would be wrong to dismiss it as 'touristy'. Similarly the other islands have their strengths and weaknesses which are best considered in cool analysis rather than simple prejudice.

Majorca

Majorca is not only the number one package-holiday destination for the British (accounting for one in eight of all package holidays sold in summer 1994), it has arguably the largest concentration of tourism in the world. After Heathrow and Gatwick, Palma airport is the third busiest international airport in Europe.

Places like Magaluf, Arenal and Palma Nova are not so much holiday resorts as holiday cities. The Majorca tourist board's statistics show that fifty per cent of the island's annual total of nearly five million visitors concentrate on this southern strip of the island. These developments take up only ten per cent of Majorca's coastline, but here there are six times more hotel beds than in the whole of Cyprus.

If Majorca is beginning to sound like the package-holiday destination from hell, don't be put off. The largest of the Balearic Islands is deceptively big: at its widest points it is sixty miles by forty – there is much more to Majorca than you could ever guess from studying a picture of the forest of tower block hotels in a tour operator's brochure.

The common perception of Majorca as a blighted, septic isle – all Rovers Return bars, sunburnt lager louts and raucous nightlife – tells just part of the story. Majorca and the package holiday appear to go together like paella and chips – but tourism to the island existed well before the malarial swamps of Magaluf yielded up a tower-block hotel.

At the beginning of the nineteenth century, the French writer George Sand and her two children travelled to Majorca with the composer Frederic Chopin, with whom she was having a secret love affair. She travelled partly to escape the gossip-mongers of Paris but mostly she went in a Wordsworthian spirit of romantic adventure.

Her party sailed from Barcelona to Majorca in November 1838. Because of the Carlist Civil War then dividing Spain, many had escaped the mainland leaving Palma overbooked and short of hotel space (a curiously familiar tale). Their failure to find suitable accommodation, combined with a failure to get along with the local people, contributed to a spectacularly disastrous visit.

In her account of the trip *Winter in Majorca* George Sand delights in the romantic landscape of Majorca but while she liked the place, she despised the people (the feeling seems to have been reciprocated). 'We nicknamed Majorca "Monkey Island" because, when surrounded by these crafty, thieving and yet innocent creatures, we grew accustomed to defending ourselves against them, but felt no more resentment or scorn than Indians feel towards chimpanzees or mischievous, timid orang-utangs.'

The suspicion with which the locals treated Sand and Chopin was largely based on the fact that Chopin was clearly suffering from the early stages of tuberculosis – a fact that Sand and Chopin chose to deny. Given Chopin's declining health, a cold damp Carthusian monastery cell in the mountain town of Valldemossa was hardly the best place to stay – particularly in winter.

While George Sand maintained a modified guerilla warfare with the Majorcans, Chopin although in failing health managed to compose – most famously the *Raindrop* prelude. ('It says here he wrote a tune about raindrops,' I heard a British visitor to the monastery tell her husband. '*Raindrops keep falling on my head*, I expect,' he replied sagely.)

As soon as they were able, the Sand/Chopin party fled home. Their visit, however, paradoxically succeeded in conferring an image of romance and bohemianism on Majorca (George Sand would properly be horrified to see how her stay with Chopin has become a major item in the island's tourist promotion.)

And in this century the island continued to attract the rich and the famous: film star Errol Flynn regularly sailed his boat along the pre-package-holiday Calvia coast. The island earned a reputation as a colony for artists and intellectuals. British writer and poet Robert Graves famously settled in Deya, a short drive from Valldemossa. (Interestingly Graves published his own translation of *Winter in Majorca* – available at the monastery shop – nicely interspersing his own waspish refutations of Sand's wilder charges against Majorca and its people.)

When the holiday business began in earnest in the Fifties, tour operators did not have to work very hard to conjure up enticing images of Majorca. In its 1957 brochure British holiday company Skytours describes the island as the 'romantic isle beloved of Chopin' (clearly even then holiday brochures were learning not to let facts get in the way of a good copy-line).

With Skytours a ten-day holiday travelling on 'daylight flights in giant four-engined Super "Hermes" aircraft' cost thirty-nine and a half guineas. The brochure promised 'gay flamenco, strumming guitars, good wine ... colourful markets where you can buy pretty but reasonably priced jewellery'.

Through the Fifties and much of the Sixties, Majorca had little to fear from tourist pollution. In 1955 the island was visited by 188,000 tourists. However, the deluge was not long in coming: the number of visitors doubled in five years – and reached a million by 1965. In 1970 the total had climbed to 1.8 million, 2.7 million in 1975, 3.3 million in 1985 before last year passing 5 million.

From the very beginning, the Majorcans themselves were able to exercise little influence over the pace of development. What the tour operators wanted, the tour operators got – throw the hotels up quickly, worry about sewage, water supply, roads and other amenities later. They wanted bed spaces, who cared about architecture or observing niceties like fire regulations?

It wasn't until post-Franco democracy took hold and the Balearic Islands became an autonomous province of Spain in the early Eighties that the Majorcan government had the power to control the growth of tourism. By then the worst of the damage was already done.

But strenuous efforts are being made to repair some of this damage. They can do little about the quality of tourist that comes but they can at least do something about the resort itself.

Magaluf and Palma Nova, which seamlessly merge, will never be mistaken for Portofino or St Tropez. They are common or garden package-holiday resorts: strips of character-less hotels backed by equally bland strips of shops and eating places to be found anywhere in the Mediterranean. (The package-holiday tourist dines on pizza and shops for leather bags, fun watches and ceramic ware.)

But while Magaluf and Palma Nova have no great aesthetic merit, Calvia council has clearly made great efforts to keep them clean and smart. Over £100 million has been earmarked for plans to attract a more up-market clientele. The major scheme is a 'Magaluf is dressing up' plan which involves building wider pavements, more pedestrianization, enlarging the promenade and planting more greenery.

By contrast in Arenal, a major resort the other side of Palma, the local council seems to have given up trying. The beach is covered with litter, many buildings have a seedy run-down look familiar to anybody who has visited the English seaside.

In its 1982 brochure Thomson described Arenal as 'Majorca's original lively resort ... a host of cafés, bars, shops and

nightspots to keep you on your toes all the time you're there ...'
Now Arenal has completely vanished from the Thomson
Summer Sun brochure. The British tourists seem to have aban-
doned the place – the bars that were once called the Queen Vic
and the Bull and Bush now have names like Pfennig and
Bavaria and attract a raucous downmarket German clientele.

But one senses that Germany, which in 1990 replaced the UK
as Majorca's leading overseas market, will soon follow the
British in rejecting cheap and nasty resorts like Arenal.

The Majorcan government has been forced to face the chal-
lenge of the future. It is laying the foundations of a policy that
stresses quality of tourism rather than quantity. The buzz-word
is 'green': green tourism, environmentally responsible tourism
– declaring conservation areas, imposing stringent regulations
on new construction, controlling sewage, restricting noise
pollution.

The island's tourism department is promoting agrotourism –
accommodation on working farms in the largely undeveloped
inland. Plans are also in hand for a host of golf courses
(although there's nothing very green about golf courses which
have a voracious thirst for scarce water resources and disfigure
the landscape).

However, there's a growing school of thought on the island
which questions whether all the island's economic eggs should
be in one tourist basket.

In the Calvia area, where the only employment used to be in
agriculture, there are now just five working farms: tourism has
become the only cash crop. Around 85 per cent of the local
economy is directly related to tourism – while the other 15 per
cent indirectly depends on the holiday trade.

Tourism has scarred Majorca but far, far less than most
people imagine. Beyond the handful of overdeveloped resorts,
Majorca has countryside as pretty as anything the
Mediterranean can offer. (Richard Branson's Virgin group,
which can spot a trend or two, has taken control of the island's
most exclusive hotel La Residencia in Deya which even with
double rooms from £200 a night continues to report brisk business. And in the days when Prince Charles and Lady Di were
still taking holidays together, summer hols with the Spanish
royal family were often taken in Majorca.)

Palma, the Majorcan capital, is also a far more attractive
place than most people imagine. 'It isn't at all what I expected,'

first-time visitors say: 'Palma's a real city – and it's so pretty.' Indeed, there's a fine harbour, handsome buildings, a striking Gothic cathedral, elegant avenues – and hardly a tower-block hotel in sight.

There are plenty of hotels – including a couple of very good hotels like the Melia Victoria – along the seafront Paseo Maritimo. But when the package-holiday business took off in the early Sixties, the bulk of the development took place outside Palma in resorts like Palma Nova, Magaluf and Arenal. So Palma has managed to remain largely a grot-free zone, which makes it an attractive base.

Within half an hour of getting off your flight (Palma is just two hours from London), you could be dipping your toes in your Palma hotel pool – or getting your teeth around a few platefuls of *tapas* in some cool backstreet bar (Palma has a surfeit of cool backstreet *tapas* bars).

If you opt to find a base on the island outside Palma, you will be spoilt for choice. Outside the overdeveloped resort strips, you could stick a pin almost anywhere and find somewhere alluring. The best-known spots include Robert Graves's home Deya. Attractive seaside places include Port D'Andratx and Port de Soller to the west, Port de Pollensa to the north and Cala D'Or to the east.

One of the beauties of Majorca is that it is so compact – from east to west it is no more than a two-hour drive. If you prefer not to drive there are good bus connections – and train services from Palma to Soller and Inca. The island is also perfect biking country: bike-hire places can be found everywhere.

Minorca

Tourist development came relatively late to Minorca when people were starting to question the wisdom of throwing up monolithic tower-block hotels. As a result Minorca, the second largest of the Balearics, has been spared the worst excesses of Magaluf or Arenal.

There are no big resorts in the Majorcan sense. For a quiet family holiday it offers the perfect environment: a collection of fine sandy beaches, good sea bathing and a wide choice of good-value accommodation and some well-planned villa developments (the island offers predominantly self-catering holidays).

The holiday places are mainly on the southern side of the banana-shaped island, where you will also find the best beaches. The best of the resorts is reckoned to be Santa Galdana, situated on an attractive horseshoe cove. It offers smart shops and a good choice of restaurants.

Many of the best beaches are off the beaten track and, unless you don't mind doing grievous bodily harm to your hired car's suspension, are best visited in a four-wheel-drive vehicle. If you are prepared to make the effort, the beach at Cala Turqueta is well worth seeking out with gorgeous fine sand and a sheltered cove.

Ibiza

During the Sixties, Ibiza won a devoted following amongst hippies and 'beautiful people'. Ibiza Town is still a popular haunt of the young in search of a good time (this tends to mean sex, drugs and rock'n'roll). But away from the throbbing nightclubs Ibiza is still a place for a good family holiday.

Playa d'en Bossa is the island's main resort. It has a good beach and a strip of hotels – but it may be too near the airport for some. Cala Vedella on the west side of the island is an attractive alternative. To the north Portinatx is also worth considering with three beaches and a relaxed atmosphere. On the east of Ibiza, Santa Eulalia del Rio is a pleasant resort with a good family atmosphere.

Formentera

Around three miles south of Ibiza, Formentera is the smallest of the Balearics: about ten miles from east to west. It is a magnet for day-trippers from Ibiza who arrive by boat and hydrofoil clutching their necessities for a day in the sun.

Water shortages have restricted the scale of tourist development on the island, so things are relatively low-key – fine if you are looking for a relatively unsophisticated holiday place.

CANARY ISLANDS

Don't look for the Canary Islands near Majorca nor anywhere else in the Mediterranean. The Canaries lie some sixty miles off the coast of the North African country of Morocco – over four hours' flying time from the UK.

Thanks to the islands' mild winter climate (they enjoy higher temperatures and less rainfall than any other European wintersun destination), they dominate the winter sun package-holiday market. And such is the Canaries' appeal, they are also starting to make their mark on the summer package market as well.

The Canaries share the same latitude as Delhi, Luxor and Florida, so one would expect them to have a reliable winter sunshine record. But a certain amount of research helps in choosing the right place for the sun: mountains and prevailing winds mean wide climatic differences – producing variations even on the same island. But even if there's plenty of winter sunshine, don't expect winter sea bathing, the sea is not so inviting – stick to the heated pool at your hotel or villa development.

The Canaries are not just sun-and-sand places (although they are perfect for this if this is what you want), they each have something individual to offer the traveller. Collectively the seven islands can come up with a dozen Blue Flag beaches and four out of the nine Spanish national parks.

The main islands for tourists are Tenerife, Gran Canaria, Lanzarote and Fuerteventura – all four are now served by direct charter flights from the UK. But it is also worth considering a holiday on one of the other three: La Gomera, La Palma and El Hierro.

Fuerteventura

This is the second largest but most scarcely populated of the Canary Islands. Its lack of population is not hard to explain: the island is arid and treeless. Its prime assets are sun and sand (152 golden beaches): useless for an agricultural lifestyle but marvellous for the tourist business.

The island is popular with two groups of people: German tourists and windsurfers (very, very popular with German windsurfers). Tourism is relatively new to Fuerteventura so facilities are not as sophisticated as they are on Tenerife or Gran Canaria.

The best of the resorts is probably Caleta de Fustes, handily placed for the airport. It's a quiet place with good apartment blocks, a fine beach and a quiet ambience for a family holiday.

Gran Canaria

This is the third largest island but the most popular with tourists. The three main resorts, San Agustin, Playa des Ingles and Maspalomas are more or less seamlessly joined together making up what is said to be the second biggest development in Spain (next to Benidorm). So with most tourists concentrated in one relatively small area, the rest of the island is fairly uncrowded.

It has some good beaches, the best of which is probably Playa del Ingles – unfortunately the resort is a bit of a concrete canyon.

Families can have a good time. Activities include wild west shows in Sioux City, camel rides on the sand dunes, shark fishing and performing parrots at Palmitos Park.

One of the most repeated phrases about Gran Canaria is that it is a 'continent in miniature'. And it does seem to have an extraordinarily rich mix of scenery: inland you can discover high mountains, quiet forests, rich valleys, coffee plantations, vineyards, avocado groves, troglodyte caves and much more.

Tenerife

Tenerife's failings are not hard to sum up: poor beaches and appalling over-development. (The beaches have ugly black volcanic sand – these have to be 'rinsed' with golden Sahara sand to make them a pleasing colour!) But these obvious faults hardly deter its devoted followers from Britain who like the busy resorts, the bustling nightlife and the exhilarating day trips up Mount Teide.

Prospective visitors should be aware of the climatic contrasts on the island. North of the mountains, the clouds they attract make Puerto de la Cruz cooler and wetter than resorts to the south. The north coast is also beachless: the authorities have built a giant lido by way of compromise.

Most visitors nowadays fly into the newer southern airport and head for the Playa de las Americas, a large bland resort of anonymous hotels and apartment blocks. But like the other main resorts on the island, it offers plenty of diversions and good nightlife aimed at the British market.

The least attractive aspect of Tenerife (as it is on several of the islands) is the time-share tout. (The secret of dealing with them is to pretend to the English touts you are German, and vice versa.)

The one excursion on Tenerife that everybody has to do is to venture to the 12,000-foot summit of Mount Teide. Happily, you don't have to pack your crampons and ice axe: a cable car shuttles you to a point 400 yards short of the summit. From the top you can see the rest of the Canary Islands and, on a clear day, the coast of Africa.

Lanzarote

In many ways Lanzarote is the most attractive of the main tourist islands. Its late start in the tourist business meant that it could learn from the mistakes made by its neighbours and has allowed tourism to develop with a more sensitive approach: highrise development has been banned.

The island after all has a remarkable environment – the effect of over 300 volcanoes. Its most striking aspect is the National Park of Timanfaya which, because of its lava and rust-coloured mountains has been compared to the spectacular scenery of Hawaii. It is claimed that American astronauts were brought here to show them what the moon would look like (although how those who brought them knew what the moon would look like isn't clear!).

The resorts all tend to be good family places. The best is probably Puerto del Carmen which offers a good uncrowded sandy beach and safe swimming. Playa Blanca in the very south is also attractive but relatively isolated: fine if you want somewhere quiet.

La Palma

This is a lush place full of banana plantations which suggests that as well as plenty of sun it gets a fair dose of rain. In appearance it is more like a Caribbean island than a Canary Island: but unlike a Caribbean island, it has few beaches – and those that it does have are volcanic black. If it isn't attractive to those who want to lie on the beach, La Palma is a perfect place fo walkers. Everyone agrees that the island's capital Santa Cruz is the most elegant of all the islands' capitals, with a number of traditional houses with decorated wooden balconies.

La Gomera

This is as far from the tourist fleshpots of Tenerife as you are likely to get. There is no airport here and no real resorts, so the only visitors it attracts are those who enjoy La Gomera's peace and quiet. It has more palm trees than all the other Canary Islands put together. It also has a Unesco World Heritage Site: the National Park of Garajonay, an ancient woodland of myrtle, ferns, laurel and giant heather trees.

El Hierro

Until Columbus discovered America, it was thought that El Hierro was the end of the world. In terms of tourism it still is. It can't offer visitors nightclubs or lidos – it doesn't have a good beach to speak of. What it does have is plenty of natural beauty and lush scenery. There is only one hotel of more than fifty rooms – and the locals would like it to stay that way!

SPAIN FOR KIDS

What is it that children like about Spain that can make a family holiday there such a wonderful experience? My children Dan and Jessica offer their own guide to the ten things they have found most memorable on their trips through Holiday Spain:

1. Orange groves
It's lovely to drive along and breathe in the sweet smell of oranges. The leaves are green and glossy. The oranges are like jewels. The fields seem to stretch for miles sometimes. It's so strange for us to see oranges, lemons and grapefruit actually growing on the trees. We're so used to picking them up from the supermarket shelves and putting them in our trolley.

2. The beaches of Galicia
We remember being the only children on these long, white stretches of sand. We scratched our names with sticks and watched the fishing boats. It was quite windy and cold because we were there at the end of October but it was sunny and the

sea was blue. We had such a happy time. On one beach there was a lot of driftwood in different shapes which we wanted to bring home. We settled for shells instead.

3. Turron

Or nougat as we call it. This is really delicious. It is usually a special sweet for Christmas but you can buy it all year round. It's made of almonds, hazelnuts, honey and sugar and cut up into small pieces. It's not hard like the nougat you get in Britain. It's handmade which makes it extra good.

4. San Sebastian

We went out for a meal one evening to a restaurant near the harbour. It was very jolly. There were masses of people laughing and walking around linked by their arms. They were dressed in colourful clothes and were going into bars. They have their dinner very late in Spain so we were hungry by the time we ate. We had fish as our main course and for pudding we had a delicious chocolate biscuit cake which was exquisite. When we came out of the restaurant all the lights were twinkling around the harbour. It was a happy night. We didn't go to bed until after 11 o'clock!

5. Santiago de Compostela

When we went into the cathedral in Santiago we were amazed to see this enormous incense burner being swung right across the heads of the congregation. It was quite frightening for us because we were only small at the time and we thought the chain would break! The incense formed clouds, you could hardly see through it. We also liked the symbol of St James which is a scallop shell. This is used on a lot of buildings as a decoration. It looks very pretty.

6. Valldemossa

The composer Chopin went with George Sand for a holiday to Majorca when he was ill with TB. He stayed in a monastery. You can still see his piano there to this day. The monastery is high on a hill and the piano had to be carried all the way up from the harbour below. It was very inspiring to see his actual piano. It also looked very delicate and fragile somehow.

7. Picos de Europa

We arrived during the month of May at the Parador of Fuente De. It was night-time. There were log fires roaring everywhere. It was very cold outside. The next morning we could hardly believe our eyes. It had snowed. It was so exciting. Unfortunately, however, we didn't have any really warm clothes with us. Anyway, we went on a cable car to the top of the mountain and quickly came back again to some hot chocolate. The view at the top was magical – and no one else was there.

8. Spanish Omelette

This is something we have quite a lot of when we are in Spain because two of our family are vegetarian. It is usually taken as a snack before the main meal. It is cold and cut into large squares. It is very filling but you always end up eating more. It's made of eggs, potatoes and onions. You can always taste the olive oil it has been cooked in. We love it!

9. The Alhambra

In the Alhambra in Granada there is the most beautiful ceiling we have ever seen. It is in the subterranean baths. The ceiling is punctured with Islamic stars and it seems as if it is night during the day. It is very pretty. The light twinkles through just as if it was a midsummer's night.

10. Colours

We love the white of the villages of Andalucia; the red dresses of the flamenco dancers, the purple of the bougainvillaea, the ochre and terracotta of the walls and the floors, the greeny grey of the olive trees and the turquoise of the sea.

8

CITY BREAKS

Spain has been a sun-and-sand destination for so long that it's sometimes hard for us to think that it can offer any other sort of holiday. In fact, it has a crop of cities ideal for short breaks. Below we discuss the merits of the three main destinations: Barcelona, Madrid and Seville – but there are many other places with direct flights that would be just as attractive: for example, Santiago de Compostela, Valencia, Oviedo or Zaragoza to name a handful. And Palma, a city served by more charter flights from the UK than any other, is a perfect place for a weekend break.

BARCELONA

It can be a big mistake to get a tune stuck in your head when you're wandering around a city – especially if it's a daft tune. I'd barely got to the beginning of La Rambla on my first morning when – pop – Freddie Mercury and Montserrat Caballe climbed uninvited into my brain to warble Barcelona (not just a daft song this, it's a song which established new horizons in pop-opera daftness).

The problem was compounded by the fact that while I had the tune (perhaps, given the song, 'tune' is pushing it a bit), I had none of the words. I had, of course, 'Barcelona ...' but then blank. I thought if I chucked in a few words of my own, perhaps this bloody tune might just go away. I began with 'Barcelona ... so good they named it twice' and somehow ended up with something that 'cleans a big, big carpet for less than half a crown'.

In fact, having a daft song spooling around my brain turned out to be not a bad accompaniment for a wander around what can be a bit of a pleasantly daft city.

Start with La Rambla, for example, where the first person I encountered was a man in his fifties dressed in a football kit clearly designed for a boy of about seven. From what I could make out of his handwritten sign (my Spanish stopped at 'O' level), he was hoping to get into the Guinness Book of Records for juggling a football from foot to foot (I think the sign said he was aiming to do it for a couple of weeks – but this may have suffered somewhat in translation). The astonishing thing about this herculean endeavour was that nobody on La Rambla seemed terribly bothered: I think the worry was that if you showed too much interest, the poor bloke might have lost concentration with awful consequences.

But if it was concentration he was after, La Rambla – in amongst the tortoise sellers, fortune tellers, shoe-shine boys, canary vendors, florists, 'find the lady' tricksters and purveyors of hard core pornography – was a daft place to be. But then that's Barcelona ('so good they named it twice ...').

If La Rambla is the first port of call in Barcelona for weekend breakers, the second is certainly the Picasso Museum housed in a couple of handsome Gothic palaces. The painter spent an important part of his life in Barcelona, between the ages of fourteen and twenty-three; which included his Blue Period.

The Museum may have few of Picasso's well-known works – *Guernica*, for example, is in Madrid – it is nevertheless a stunning collection which shows the painter's extraordinary development as an artist: from early competent but unremarkable youthful sketches to his impressive studies on a theme by Velazquez.

The only wearing aspect of the museum is that it tends to fill up with coach parties of people 'doing' Europe. Two elderly American ladies were pondering one of the Harlequin paintings. 'Perhaps we could get it from the gift shop,' said one. 'What? A print of *this*!' croaked her friend in horror. 'No, that Picasso per*fume*: Paloma ... you know.'

'He made per*fume* too? Some hell of a guy, Peggy.'

Barcelona's other must-see cultural attraction is the work of architect Antonio Gaudi. I felt about Gaudi the same doubts I have about Salvador Dali: man of genius – or just daft as a brush? A visit to Gaudi's best-known work: the Sagrada Familia church pushed me into the 'man of genius' camp.

I knew that the church was unfinished; I hadn't realized quite how unfinished – it's more building site than place of worship. All that exists are the walls and the spires, but these amount to rather a lot. A climb up to the top of one of the eight spires is not lightly undertaken, but is recommended in order to have a close look at the extraordinary detailing which reveals the trademark organic forms. The sunflower tops to the spires are like a joyful shout of praise, irrepressible and, well, slightly daft.

Having enjoyed the Sagrada Familia you will probably wish to seek out the other famous Gaudi buildings: the Casa Mila or La Pedrera, on Passeig de Gracia, with its extraordinary flowing balconies; the Casa Batllo, also on Passeig de Gracia, with its eyecatching ceramics – and Palau Guell near La Rambla. Also worth the trip is the Gaudi House Museum in Parc Guell with its gingerbread houses and dragon slides.

In contrast to his exuberant architecture, Gaudi's death was improbably bleak: when in 1926 he was run over by a tram and killed, he had become a virtual recluse. Once something of a dandy, he was found at the scene of the accident barefoot in his shoes, his jacket held together by safety pins. A fascinating exhibition on Gaudi's life and work in the crypt of the Sagrada Familia shows that almost the whole of Barcelona turned out to join his funeral procession. (Hard to think of the death of a modern British architect which would induce a similar public display of grief.)

Shortly after Gaudi's death Barcelona was plunged into the sort of social turmoil familiar today from newsreel footage of Bosnia. In 1931 a Catalan Republic was proclaimed in Barcelona: for the next eight years, until the city fell, to Franco's fascist army, Barcelona was riven by faction fighting between assorted groups of socialists, communists and anarchists (a struggle wonderfully recorded by George Orwell in *Homage to Catalonia*).

Barcelona's resurrection as one of the great cities of Europe was completed when the city hosted the 1992 Olympic games with stylish self-confidence. It's worth taking a trip up the hill of Montjuic just to take a look at the Olympic stadium. The Joan Miro Foundation is to be found here, there is also an amusement park, as well as a Spanish village which has examples of architecture and craft-manship from all over the country.

Finish your visit to Barcelona down at the bottom end of La Rambla next to the harbour, looking up at the huge Columbus monument, topped by a statue of the great explorer pointing out to sea. The statue was raised for the universal exhibition of

1888 when it was argued that Columbus was really a Catalan (a hopelessly daft idea).

Now a new tune popped into my mind: 'They all laughed at Christopher Columbus when he said the world was round ...' Grateful to be free of Freddie Mercury, I trotted back up La Rambla to see how my friend the football juggler was doing. On second look not daft, I decided, just very deft. Like Barcelona.

MADRID

The Spanish capital is one of those happy places for tourists where they can largely forget about the intricate details of sightseeing – there are few major sights to see. Here they can simply concentrate on absorbing the ambience and devote themselves to having a good time.

Its lack of historical sights can be partly explained by its lack of history. Madrid was chosen as capital in 1561 by Philip II because of its geographical position at the heart of Spain. Its location is certainly not ideal from other points of view: its position on a high plateau (at 2100ft above sea level, it is surprisingly Europe's highest capital) means that it is too cold in winter and too hot in summer.

On the face of things it would seem to have little going for it as a short-break place. However, it is in many ways a surprisingly attractive city. It may lack the grand civic architecture of Vienna but it more than makes up for this with a noticeable *joie de vivre* – Madrid people are renowned for late nights. The city has an excellent Metro system which makes it cheap and easy to get around.

The heart of the city is the Puerta del Sol which sits at the hub of ten converging streets. This is also the heart of Spain: a stone slab notes the fact that this is Kilometre Zero – from here all road distances from Madrid are measured. It is also the main shopping centre with branches of the department stores El Corte Ingles and Galerias Preciados.

Another significant meeting place is the Plaza Mayor, once the scene of bullfights and inquisition trials, but which now boasts a fine selection of restaurants and good-value *tapas* bars.

The one sight that all visitors have heard of, and will want to visit, is the Prado which houses one of the world's finest art collections. The collection is so vast (1000 works are on display) that you need to plan your visit with some care: buy an English guidebook to the museum and plot your course in advance. There are good collections of works by Velazquez and Goya – and some fascinating paintings by El Greco. One of the best known works on display is Velazquez's *Las Meninas* (The Ladies-in-Waiting). Other artists represented in the Prado include Raphael, Titian, Tintoretto and Bosch (including his famous *The Garden of Earthly Delights*).

Madrid's most famous work of art hangs in the Cason del Buen Retiro, south of the Prado. Picasso's *Guernica* is a symbolic representation of the German bombing of the Basque town of Guernica on 26 April 1937 when 2000 civilians were killed. Picasso decreed that the painting should never hang in Spain until democracy had been restored. It was finally brought to Spain in 1981, after Picasso's death.

The other major attraction is the Royal Palace which has 2800 rooms: you will be pleased to hear that only some of them are open to the public.

One of the attractions of a short break in Madrid is that there are a number of fascinating places within a relatively short distance. Segovia, El Escorial and Toledo are all within easy reach.

SEVILLE

In the same year that the Olympics were held in Barcelona, Seville also took its place on the international stage as the venue for Expo 92. The year of 1992 was taken as Spain's year because it marked the 500th anniversary of Columbus's discovery of the New World.

For visitors to the Expo, there was the chance to rediscover Seville, a city that had curiously dropped beneath many travellers' horizons. Its re-emergence is welcome because Seville is a genuine treasure, offering an exciting contrast to Barcelona.

Seville has been snootily described as a city famous for its oranges and its women. For all that the Catalans might complain about the indolence and slothfulness of the south, the Andalucian capital is a place of great passion and surprising energy. It is after all the city of *Carmen*: dark, mysterious and rather hot-blooded. It is also the city of *Fidelio, Don Giovanni,*

The Marriage of Figaro and, of course, *The Barber of Seville* (what other city in the world can claim to be the subject of five of the world's greatest operas!).

Seville's supreme attraction for the weekend breaker is that the main centre is wonderfully compact, easily visited in two days (if you take it at a canter, one full day will do you).

If you find the idea of 'doing' the sights daunting, Seville is perfect for idle wandering. There is no official policy of pedestrianization: happily the streets were built to accommodate more sedate transport than the motor car (they were also built close together to heighten the shade and diminish the baking heat of summer).

For centuries Seville had a lead role on the world stage. During its Golden Age, people of the city said 'Madrid is the capital of Spain but Seville is the capital of the world.' Its monopoly trade with the New World brought the city untold wealth. Given that Seville had already established huge prosperity from a busy trade with a succession of traders dating back to the Romans and before, it is easy to understand the prosperous look of the place. (Times, of late, have been hard: like the rest of Andalucia, Seville suffers high unemployment. This helps explain why petty crime is a particular problem in Seville: be on the lookout for bag snatchers.)

Its rich history has left a legacy of marvellous buildings. The Great Mosque of Seville was razed to the ground in 1401 to make way for the huge cathedral. Fortunately the mosque's Giralda still remains, standing beside the cathedral. The cathedral is the final resting place for King Ferdinand III who delivered Seville from the Moors. There is also a huge 19th-century monument to Christopher Columbus here.

The most intriguing tourist attraction is the Alcazar, originally built by the Arab rulers but after the Christian conquest it became a residence for the Spanish kings, notably Pedro the Cruel.

Other places worth a look include the Fabrica de Tabacos, the city's old tobacco factory – the setting for Bizet's *Carmen* – but now part of the city's university.

After dark, search out a club that offers genuine spontaneous *flamenco* (rather than the staged rather soulless variety).

9
DIRECTORY OF SPANISH
SPECIALIST TOUR OPERATORS

For each operator we show whether it is a member of ABTA (Association of British Travel Agents), has an Air Tour Organiser's Licence (ATOL), and whether it belongs to the Association of Independent Tour Operators (AITO): all of which guarantee that a company is bonded. Under European legislation all companies offering package travel should offer such protection but the law is patchily enforced – it would be wise to check with any operator before booking. For all purchases over £100 made with a credit card (Access or Visa only), you are protected under the Consumer Credit Act. If the operator goes bust you can recover your money from the credit card company. As well as a brief description of each company, the listing shows which credit cards it accepts and under which other sections of this book you can find more information about the holidays it offers.

3D Golf plc
62 Viewfield Road,
Ayr KA8 8HH
Admin: 0292 263331
Res: 0292 263331
Fax: 0292 286424
ABTA: 69078 ATOL: 1815
Visa, Access, Switch
'3D is a golf specialist tour operator. It was established in 1976 and carries around 10,000 passengers annually. Destinations featured are the Costa del Sol and Almeria. It is an independent company run by golfers for golfers.'
Special interest holidays: Golf

AA Driveaway
AA Motoring Holidays,
Automobile Association Developments, PO Box 128
Fanum House,
Basingstoke RG21 2AE
Admin: 0256 493878
Res: 0256 493878
ABTA: 65626
Visa, Access
The AA in its Driveaway programme offers short breaks and hotel touring holidays. 'As well as the ferry crossing, we book all your chosen hotels in advance. You can book as many hotels as

you like and stay in each hotel as long as you wish. You can also add on extra nights with any of the other hotel groups or countries in our brochure. Another option is our go-as-you-please programme. Here we only book your ferry crossing and you take nightly vouchers belonging to the same hotel group.'
Hotel holidays: All over Spain

Abercrombie & Kent
Sloane Square House, Holbein Place, London SW1W 8NS
Admin: 071-730 9600
Res: 071-730 9600
Fax: 071-730 9376
ABTA: 72314
Visa, Access, Amex, Diners
'Abercrombie & Kent has been in business since 1962 and offers travel for a small and select clientele. It consciously seeks out those destinations which are out of the ordinary and are set apart from the run-of-the-mill. In Spain it offers Andalucian Safaris – walks in the Sierras.'
Special interest holidays: Walking and trekking

Aeroscope
Scope House, Hospital Road, Moreton-in-Marsh, Glos GL56 0BQ
Admin: 0608 50103
Res: 0608 50103
Fax: 0608 51295
ABTA: 74061 ATOL: 1377

Visa, Access
'Aeroscope has been established for nearly fourteen years and is fully bonded and licensed with ABTA, IATA and the CAA. It caters for holidaymakers and travellers who primarily are independently-minded and like to do their own thing. Aeroscope is a provider of competitive air fares throughout Europe and provides accommodation, if required, in any one of 800 Best Western hotels as well as a wide choice of youth and family hostels for the budget conscious.'
Special interest holidays: City breaks

Airtours
Wavell House, Holcombe Road, Helmshore, Rossendale BB4 4NB
Admin: 0706 830130
Res: 0706 260000
ATOL: 1379
Visa, Access
Britain's second largest tour operator.
Hotel holidays: All over Spain
Self-catering holidays: All over Spain

Allegro Holidays
Vanguard House, 277 London Road, Burgess Hill, West Sussex RH15 9QU
Admin: 0444 248222
Res: 0444 248222
Fax: 0444 235789

128

ABTA: 12173
ATOL: 1835
AITO
Visa, Access, Amex
'Allegro Holidays has operated for more than ten years. It offers year-round holidays to the Canary Islands, using convenient day flights from Gatwick. The company features a choice of quality hotels and apartments on Tenerife, Lanzarote and Gran Canaria.'
Hotel holidays: Canary Islands
Self-catering holidays: Canary Islands

Alternative Travel Group
69–71 Banbury Road,
Oxford OX2 6PE
Admin: 0865 310399
Res: 0865 310399
Fax: 0865 310299
ATOL: 2618
AITO
Visa, Access
'In 1979 the company launched a new concept and style of travelling: journeys on foot through the most beautiful and interesting parts of Europe, with comfortable, characteristic accommodation, good food and wine, a wide spectrum of interests and luggage transported *en route.* Each trip is accompanied by a deluxe Mercedes minibus, so clients can walk as much or as little as they like, and two highly trained staff. Small groups (never more than sixteen people) walk along carefully researched routes which include the best views, the most picturesque paths, the rarest and most profuse wild flowers and opportunities to see interesting birds and animals as well as the finest art and architecture. A day with – say – five hours of walking might involve starting at 9.00am, and with time to enjoy everything *en route,* and an hour and a half for lunch and a siesta, you could expect to arrive at the next hotel at about 4.30pm. We walk at an even pace that seems to suit most people.'
Special interest holidays: Walking and trekking

Angela Holidays
Oaktree House, Lowford,
Bursledon,
Southampton SO3 8ES
Admin: 0703 404536
Res: 0703 403866
Fax: 0703 406470
Visa, Access
'Angela Holidays has been bonded with the Bus and Coach Council Bonded Holiday Section since 1981. In Spain it offers holidays to the Costa Brava, Cantabria, and an eleven-day tour of Madrid, Seville, Jerez, Gibraltar and Granada.'
Special interest holidays: Coach holidays

Anglers World Holidays

46 Knifesmithgate,
Chesterfield,
Derbyshire S40 1RQ
Admin: 0246 221717
Res: 0246 221717
Fax: 0246 824515
ABTA: 42639
Visa, Access

'Anglers World is Britain's largest specialist angling holiday operator. It provides each client with a comprehensive guide, full of angling information prepared by a team of experts. Maps are also supplied. Destinations include Ireland, Holland, Denmark, Sweden and Spain. Family fishing holidays are featured. These combine good fishing with a range of activities for the family.'

Special interest holidays:
Angling

Arblaster & Clarke Wine Tours

104 Church Road, Steep,
Petersfield GU32 2DD
Admin: 0730 266883
Res: 0730 266883
Fax: 0730 268620
ATOL: 2543
AITO
Visa, Access

'Arblaster & Clarke is an independent, family firm which has been trading since Autumn 1986. It is fully bonded with AITO and through its CAA ATOL licence. As it is a small, specialist firm, the office staff are all well-informed and are also tour managers. Having first-hand experience of the tours, they know the hotels and are able to answer any questions you may have. The tours are well organized and the wine guides (often Masters of Wine) are outgoing experts who communicate their knowledge in an infectious, intelligent or amusing way. Each tour is also accompanied by a multilingual, experienced tour manager. The atmosphere on the tours is always friendly and informal. Visits are often to leading wine estates where we have a very warm welcome. These visits often include meals at the chateau with the owner or the winemaker. This is something that an individual cannot arrange for himself. Where we include other meals, these are always special and with good wines. Our carefully chosen hotels are hotels of character and charm, and well located. Areas covered in Spain include Rioja and northern Spain, Barcelona, Seville and Jerez.'

Special interest holidays: Wine tours

Artscape Painting Holidays

Suite 4, Hamlet Court
Business Centre,
18 Hamlet Court Road,
Westcliff-on-Sea SS0 7LX
Admin: 0702 435990
Res: 0702 435990
Visa, Access

'Artscape offers a choice of sixty courses, each one carefully planned to suit the centre and with a course programme for artists with a range of interests and talents. We offer a choice of locations, tutors and courses. If you enjoy being with a certain tutor, you can join him or her at a different place each year. There is an extensive range of courses – modern and traditional, portrait and landscape for foundation and advanced students. Our painting groups are seldom more than fifteen, never more than twenty. Non-painting partners are welcome.'

Special interest holidays: Painting and drawing holidays

A T Mays City Breaks

21 Royal Crescent,
Glasgow G3 7SZ
Admin: 041 331 1200
Res: 041 331 1121
Fax: 041 332 0563
ABTA: 49712
ATOL: 0020
Visa, Access, Amex, Diners
'City Breaks is a division of A T Mays, the fourth largest multiple travel agent in the UK. It has been established for six years. We carry over 10,000 passengers every year to twenty-three destinations including Rome, Florence and Venice. Our clients can choose to concentrate on seeing one city or combine two or three destinations in a multi-centre holiday. Our packages include scheduled flight departures from twenty-five UK airports and hotel accommodation in a range of categories, from two-star to five-star deluxe. Our hotels are all centrally located and we can also arrange reasonably priced excursions. For groups of ten or more people travelling together, our Groups Department organizes departures to all our city-break destinations.'

Special interest holidays: City breaks

Aventura

Aptdo 21, Orgiva, Granada, Spain
Admin: 010 34 58 785253
No credit cards accepted.
'Aventura has been trading since 1971. It is a family-run business and carries around 100 to 150 people annually. It features trail riding on horseback in the Sierra Nevada and Alpujarras areas. Long-distance rides and special expeditions in the mountains are also organized.'

Special interest holidays: Horseriding

Beach Villas Holidays

8 Market Passage,
Cambridge CB2 3QR
Admin: 0223 311113
Res: 0223 311113

Fax: 0223 313577
ABTA: 1415
ATOL: 2776
AITO
Visa, Access, Amex, Switch
'Established since 1970, Beach Villas operates a specialized programme to a variety of locations in Spain. The main areas include Majorca, Minorca, Costa Brava, Costa Blanca, Costa del Sol and the Canary Islands. The programme is exclusively self-catering, in resorts that will suit families looking for a quieter type of holiday. The company carries around 60,000 passengers annually with a heavy emphasis on villa-type holidays, most of which require and receive a half-price car. The company prides itself on a high level of repeat business and a low level of complaints. The company is privately owned and sells holidays direct and through ABTA agents. All families receive excellent child reductions which include free places (now limited to low-season months) or a fifty per cent discount for children. All other children also qualify for reductions provided they are accompanying two full-fare paying passengers.'
Self-catering holidays: Balearic Islands, Catalonia, Valencia, Canary Islands

Bike Tours
82 Walcot Street,
Bath BA1 1BX
Admin: 0225 480130
Res: 0225 480130
Fax: 0225 480132
ATOL: 2943
Visa, Access
'We have traded for two years as Bike Tours. Formerly tours were administered by Bike Events which now specializes in day and weekend events. We take about 200 people to Spain annually, and many more worldwide. We have mountain biking holidays in the Pyrenees. With groups of four or five there's plenty of individual attention. We also have an annual tour running from Bordeaux through the Pyrenees and via Montserrat to Barcelona. This takes place over two weeks in September and attracts around 120 people. Our tours enjoy a special place in cycle tourists' affections for their care-fully researched routes and amazing atmosphere. Route sheets enable cyclists to go at their own pace; the roving mechanic and nurse take care of any problems. There's also a van to pick up anyone who wants a lift. The tea tent, with its wonderful spread of bread and cakes is a magnet for cyclists bursting to tell tales of the day's astonishing feats of endurance, stoicism and

general derring-do in the face of large lunches and vino tinto. On a Bike Tours holiday almost anything can happen – and it usually does.'
Special interest holidays:
Cycling holidays

Birding

Periteau House, Winchelsea, East Sussex TN36 4EA
Admin: 0797 223223
Res: 0797 223223
Fax: 0797 222911
ATOL: 2922

'Birding has over ten years of organizing bird holidays. It is the only tour operator ranked 'Excellent' by *British Birds* in both 1986 and 1992. Groups have a maximum of sixteen participants, often fewer and all the leaders are experienced and expert. Birding contributes to international conservation in a variety of ways from cash donations to physical help. Over the past year it has given £450 to the Spanish Steppes Appeal of ICBP to help purchase a reserve to act as the centrepiece of efforts to save the Great Bustard. Birding holidays are suitable for all levels of birdwatching ability from virtual beginners to fully fledged experts. The company is also flexible enough to accommodate the needs of the non-birding partner and is happy to advise whether or not a tour is suitable.'

Special interest holidays:
Birdwatching

Brittany Ferries

The Brittany Centre, Wharf Road, Portsmouth PO2 8RU
Admin: 0705 892200
Res: 0705 827701
Fax: 0705 892204
Visa, Access, Amex, Diners, Switch

'Brittany Ferries has been trading for twenty-one years and has grown from a turnover of £700,000 to £210 million. The company operates ferry services from Portsmouth, Poole and Plymouth to western France and Santander in northern Spain. It carries more than 50 per cent of passengers travelling across the western Channel. The service to Santander began in 1978 and carried 140,000 people in 1993 whilst overall nearly three million people travelled on one of our nine ships during the same year. Our inclusive holidays and breaks to Spain concentrate on Cantabria and Asturias, better known as the Costa Verde. The remainder of Spain can be visited by taking one of our touring holidays and for those loving the Mediterranean coast there is a selection of villas on the Costa Blanca.'
Hotel holidays: Valencia, Galicia, Cantabria/Asturias

Self-catering holidays:
Cantabria/Asturias, Valencia,
Catalonia
Special interest holidays:
Paradores and pousadas

CV Travel
43 Cadogan Street, London
SW3 2PR
Admin: 071-581 0851
Res: 071-581 0851
Fax: 071-584 5229
ABTA: 23290
ATOL: 337
AITO
Visa, Access

'For over twenty years, CV Travel has been following a pioneering philosophy of arranging holidays that are uniquely different. As an owner-managed company we remain fiercely independent. We strive for, and are able to achieve high levels of personalized service, quality and flexibility. Our 1994 Mediterranean World programme offers a selection of villas and hotels in Italy, Portugal and particularly Spain. We carry about 7500 passengers a year. In Spain we concentrate on areas away from the Costas, covering predominantly inland areas in both Andalucia and Majorca. In both locations we offer high-quality villas with private swimming pools. We also have one villa on Minorca. Our hotels, like our villas, are away from the main tourist areas. We offer some uniquely individual hotels in Andalucia and the very well-known La Residencia in Majorca.'

Hotel holidays: Andalucia, Balearic Islands
Self-catering holidays:
Andalucia, Balearic Islands

Caravan & Camping Service
69 Westbourne Grove,
London W2 4UJ
Admin: 071-792 1944
Res: 071-792 1944
Fax: 071-792 1956
AITO
Visa, Access, Switch

'Established in 1986, Caravan & Camping Service offers a specialist advance campsite reservation service for the owners of touring caravans, trailer tents, tents or motor caravans. The company offers a high degree of personal service and expert, friendly advice on route planning and site selection, from staff members who have visited each site. In addition to the Costa Brava, Asturias and Cantabria in Spain over 130 sites are available in eight European countries. Customers can either sail direct to and from Spain or visit campsites in France *en route*. Each holiday is tailormade to suit the customer's requirements, for either site-only reservations or ferry-inclusive holidays. The ferry-inclusive package price, for site reservations and ferry crossings can give considerable savings on booking the holiday independently.'

Special interest holidays: Caravans and mobile homes, Camping

Casas Cantabricas
31 Arbury Road,
Cambridge CB4 2JB
Admin: 0223 328721
Res: 0223 328721
Fax: 0223 322711
AITO
Visa, Access
'Casas Cantabricas offers self-catering and pension holidays in the north of Spain – in Cantabria and Asturias, including the Picos de Europa and in La Coruna province, Galicia. We have a wide choice of locally owned properties, from cottages to "palacio", old farmhouses to modern apartments. Locations vary too, from seaside to mountain, countryside to village or small town. We are an independent family business established in 1985, and the first to offer *gite* holidays in northern Spain. We have developed and are proud of our local knowledge and the personal service this enables us to offer. We send about 1500 people on holiday annually – many come back or send their friends. '

Hotel holidays: Cantabria/ Asturias
Self-catering holidays: Cantabria/Asturias, Galicia

Castaways
2-10 Cross Road,
Tadworth KT20 5UJ
Admin: 0737 814300
Res: 0737 812255
Fax: 0737 814465
ABTA: 18466
ATOL: 1140
Visa, Access, Amex, Diners, Switch
'Castaways offers holidays to the quieter regions of the island of Majorca. Since 1979, many thousands of clients have enjoyed staying in the many varied hotels which are located in mountain villages and at small places by the sea. Our hotels range from simple, family-owned pensions to grand-luxe establishments. Many of these are ideal for families and reductions for children sharing with parents can be 60 per cent. Flights are from every UK airport. All transfers are by private car.'
Hotel holidays: Balearic Islands

Celtic Holidays
94 King Street, Maidstone,
Kent ME14 1BH
Admin: 0622 690009
Res: 0622 690009
Fax: 0622 691557
ATOL: 1772
No credit cards accepted

'The company has been specializing in holidays to Minorca for over eighteen years and offers villa, apartment, residencia, hotel and farmhouse holidays. Clients can fly from a local airport on a day flight with a flight duration of between two and three hours depending on departure airport. Our properties vary from self-catering to bed and breakfast to full board. Self-catering apartments are near the beach and many have shared pools. There are also villas with private pools or without a pool but only fifty metres from the beach. The hotels are good quality three-star hotels and the catered farmhouse holiday offers an unusual alternative.'
Hotel holidays: Balearic Islands
Self-catering holidays: Balearic Islands

Classic Collection Holidays
Wiston House, 1 Wiston Avenue, Worthing BN14 7QL
Admin: 0903 823088
Res: 0903 823088
Fax: 0903 214945
ABTA: 2505
ATOL: 2475
Visa, Access, Amex
'Classic Collection Holidays has been trading for six years. It is a small, independent specialist tour operator featuring Majorca, Tenerife, La Gomera, La Palma, Madeira and Cyprus. It carries approximately 500 passengers a year. It offers holidays designed for the independently minded traveller, with the freedom to go their own way and explore at their own pace.'
Hotel holidays: Balearic Islands

Club Med
106/110 Brompton Road, London SW3 1JJ
Admin: 071-581 1161
Res: 071-581 1161
Fax: 071-581 4769
ABTA: 19685
ATOL: 1020
Visa, Access, Amex
Club Med has been trading for forty-three years. 'Our Summer 94 brochure offers eighty-two villages in thirty countries, all different in style and atmosphere. Every village is a self-sufficient community with all your holiday needs 'on-site' including: accommodation, restaurants, bars, a boutique, medical care, a bank, sports facilities, children's clubs and entertainment. Our prices are all fully inclusive. Our prices include full board, meals with wine, insurance, sports activities, sports tuition, return flights or trains and transfers, children's clubs, evening shows and nightclubs.'
Special interest holidays: Club Holidays

Club Pollensa Holidays
7 Warwick Street, Worthing,
West Sussex BN11 3DF
Admin: 0903 230128
Res: 0903 200237
Fax: 0903 201225
ABTA: 928
Visa, Access, Amex, Diners,
Switch
'Club Pollensa offers a choice
of countryside villas with
pools, apartments and hotels
on the north coast of Majorca.'
Hotel holidays: Balearic Islands
Self-catering holidays: Balearic
Islands

Connexions
Atlas Partnership, Clock
House, High Street, Cuckfield,
West Sussex RH17 5LB
Admin: 0444 417299
Res: 0444 417299
Fax: 0444 414499
ATOL: 3177
Visa, Access, Amex, Diners,
Switch
Connexions is a trading divi-
sion of Atlas Partnership. It
offers villas, apartments, hotel
and hotel apartments at the
La Manga Club in Murcia.
Hotel holidays: Murcia
Self-catering holidays: Murcia

Corona Holidays of London
73 High Road, South
Woodford, London E18 2QP
Admin: 081-530 3747
Res: 081-530 2500
Fax: 081-530 3636
ABTA: 20432

AITO
Visa, Access, Amex
'Alan and Janet Cornish,
owners of Corona Holidays of
London, have been going to
the Canaries for over twenty
years. Their brochure is their
personal selection of villas,
apartments and hotels. There
are considerable differences
within it – lively and quiet
resorts, luxury developments
with many facilities and
simple, economy standard
apartments. The owners of the
company have stayed at all
the accommodation featured
and all comments and des-
criptions are based upon their
personal experience.'
Hotel holidays: Canary Islands
Self-catering holidays: Canary
Islands
Special interest holidays:
Paradors and pousadas

Cosmosair
Tourama House, 17
Homesdale Road, Bromley,
Kent BR2 9LX
Admin: 061 480 9996
Res: 061 480 5799
Fax: 061 480 0833
ABTA: 23318
ATOL: 2275
Visa, Access
'Cosmos is part of a major,
Swiss-owned, international
travel organization with inter-
ests worldwide. In the UK the
group includes Avro plc, a
large flight-only operator, and

Monarch Airlines, one of the country's leading independent charter airlines. Overseas, the group owns Globus Gateway, the largest organization of European coach touring holidays in the world, with a strong presence in the North American market. Established more than thirty years ago, Cosmos is one of the UK's leading and longest-running tour operators and has been offering holidays to Italy since its inception across a range of products to suit every taste and budget. The Cosmos air and coach programmes together carry in excess of 500,000 passengers annually. Most areas of Italy are included in one or more of the different holiday brochures. Of special interest to the family market is Cosmos Sunlink, offering top-value hotels and apartments where children can travel free or enjoy large reductions on the adult price as well as taking advantage of the new Sooty Club which offers supervised fun for children aged two to ten at all Sunlink hotels. Cosmos also offers free local departures from over 290 pick-up points throughout the UK.'
Hotel holidays: All over Spain
Self-catering holidays: All over Spain
Special interest holidays: Coach holidays

Discover the World
The Flatt Lodge, Bewcastle,
Near Carlisle,
Cumbria CA6 6PH
Admin: 06977 48361
Res: 06977 48361
Fax: 06977 48327
ABTA: 1366
ATOL: 2896
AITO
Visa, Access
'Discover the World is a unique travel company that works exclusively with conservation organizations to create special programmes of wildlife and wilderness holidays for their members. A significant proportion of its income is donated to conservation projects around the world. It is the sister company to Arctic Experience, the UK specialist to the Arctic and Sub-Arctic. We offer a wide choice of tours ranging from weekend wilderness breaks to complex expeditions lasting for several weeks. These are designed to be informative, as well as great fun, and are based on well-planned itineraries that have been thoroughly researched beforehand.'
Special interest holidays:
Natural history

Enterprise
Owners Abroad House, Peel Cross Road, Salford,
Manchester M5 2AN

Admin: 061-745 4633
Res: 061-745 7000
Fax: 061-745 4533
ABTA: 68342
ATOL: 230
Visa, Access
Enterprise is part of the Owners Abroad Group, Britain's second largest holiday company. It has its own airline Air 2000 which handles most of its holiday flights.

Euro Academy
77a George Street, Croydon, Surrey CRO 1LD
Admin: 081-680 4618
Res: 081-686 2363
Fax: 081-681 8850
ABTA: 6910
Visa, Access, Amex
'Euro Academy offers you the benefit of its twenty-three years' experience arranging quality language courses "on location" in Europe. Euro Academy is a small independent operator providing a wide range of courses. General courses offer a leisurely approach. Visits and excursions complement the tuition. There is a good range of activities provided, including Sevillana dances, Spanish cuisine, traditional Flamenco and fiestas. General courses are for all ages, all levels, all year. Duration is from two or three weeks up to twelve weeks. Intensive courses offer the chance to make the best use of limited time in the environment of small groups or one to one. Individual tuition is for all levels with durations from one week. It is ideal for students about to sit examinations and for adults. Courses are based in Madrid, Malaga, Nerja, Seville, Salamanca, Valencia and Barcelona.'
Special interest holidays:
Language learning

Eurocamp Travel
28 Princess Street, Knutsford, Cheshire WA16 6BG
Admin: 0565 626262
Res: 0565 626262
ABTA: 70677
AITO
Visa, Access
'Eurocamp is a self-drive camping holiday operator and was established twenty-one years ago. It offers holidays in pre-erected tents and mobile homes in thirteen European countries on 270 sites. The travel arrangements service ensures flexibility – clients can stay for as many or as few nights as they wish and travel on any day of the week. Nearly 80 per cent of holidays last year were taken by past customers and friends.'
Special interest holidays:
Camping

European Villas
154–156 Victoria Road,
Cambridge CB4 3DZ
Admin: 0223 314220
Res: 0223 314220
Fax: 0223 314423
ABTA: 99694
ATOL: 2270
AITO
Visa, Access, Amex
'Cambridge-based European Villas is a privately owned tour operator specializing in quality villas, all with private pools. It carried around 15,000 people in 1993. European Villas has been steadily expanding its portfolio of properties, and whilst the Company also features the Algarve, France, Cyprus, Corfu, Gozo and Tuscany, Spain was where the operation started ten years ago, and Spain remains the largest portfolio of properties, covering the Costa Blanca, Catalonia, Ibiza, Majorca and Minorca. All villas are contracted personally by the Directors with a view to both interior quality and comfort, location, views, tranquillity and character. The brochure grades each villa, including a deluxe category. The holidays are offered on a rental-only basis or inclusive of flights from over ten UK airports, with child discounts on all dates, and unlimited free child places available.

Additional services include car hire, welcome food packs, maid service, video and TV hire, highchairs, playpens, coolbags etc.'
Self-catering holidays:
Catalonia, Valencia, Balearic Islands

EuroSites
Wavell House, Holcombe Road, Helmshore,
Rossendale BB4 4NB
Admin: 0706 830888
Res: 0706 830888
Fax: 0706 830248
Visa, Access
EuroSites is part of the Airtours Group. It offers camping and mobile-home holidays throughout Europe.
Special interest holidays:
Camping

Excalibur
221 Old Christchurch Road,
Bournemouth,
Dorset BH1 1PG
Admin: 0202 701123
Res: 0202 701123
Fax: 0202 701133
ABTA: 8227
Visa, Access
'Excalibur is an independent company. It has been sales agent for the Al-Andalus Express, Spain's luxury train, since 1991.'
Special interest holidays: Train holidays

Exodus

9 Weir Road,
London SW17 0LT
Admin: 081-675 5550
Res: 081-675 5550
Fax: 081-673 0779
ATOL: 2582
AITO
Visa, Access, Amex

'Exodus has been established for more than twenty years as an operator offering walking and adventure holidays. The directors of Exodus today have been with the company since its conception in 1973. In 1979, Exodus introduced its walking programme and later in 1982, a range of adventure trips. During that time the company has developed programmes to meet the demands of those who want more out of their holiday than sun and sea, but do not always have the time for longer expeditions.'

Special interest holidays:
Adventure holidays

Explore Worldwide

1 Frederick Street, Aldershot, Hants GU11 1LQ
Admin: 0252 344161
Res: 0252 319448
Fax: 0252 343170
ATOL: 2595
AITO
Visa, Access, Switch

'Explore Worldwide has been offering small group adventure holidays for more than thirteen years. The average group size is sixteen people, led by a tour leader, allowing us flexibility and a real opportunity to discover more about the places we visit. We often use a variety of transport to suit the area we are travelling in – this could be a local train, a chartered bus, a donkey or on foot. Different types of accommodation are used on different trips but we usually aim to stay in small, comfortable hotels chosen for their charm and atmosphere. Most trips are on a bed and breakfast basis, offering the opportunity to try the local food and experiment with restaurants and cuisine. Sometimes we combine hotels with more basic accommodation such as mountain refuges or simple guesthouses where this is the only accommodation available, and occasionally, where desirable, we camp. We aim to see the main sites of interest, but also the lesser known places, away from mainstream tourism, the quiet backroads and friendly villages. We welcome families with children fourteen years and over. In our worldwide brochure we offer three different itineraries to Spain – a walking trip in the Sierra Nevada in southern Spain, cultural and adventure touring in Andalucia, and

hiking in the Picos de Europa in Asturias, northern Spain. Trips in Spain range from eight days to fifteen days and offer active people the opportunity to get to know the real Spain.'
Special interest holidays: Walking and trekking

Flightline
28 Ironmarket, Newcastle-under-Lyme,
Staffordshire ST5 1RH
Admin: 0782 717002
Res: 0782 639833
ATOL: 2256
An independent tour operator offering hotel and self-catering accommodation in the Canary Islands.
Hotel holidays: Canary Islands
Self-catering holidays: Canary Islands

Fourwinds Holidays
Bearland House, Longsmith Street, Gloucester GL1 2HL
Admin: 0452 524151
Res: 0452 527656
Fax: 0452 419312
ABTA: 23360
ATOL: 1638
Visa, Access, Amex, Diners
'Cotswold Fourwinds has been trading for thirteen years, based in the Gloucester area. It is a predominantly European coaching tour operator, but in the last few years it has organized a number of longhaul products, for

example, West Coast USA, Thailand and Canada. The company forms part of Cannon Street Investments plc and it carries approximately 55,000 passengers annually.'
Special interest holidays: Coach holidays

H20 Holidays
3 Trafalgar Gate, Brighton Marina, Brighton,
Sussex BN2 5UU
Admin: 0273 819999
Res: 0273 819999
Fax: 0273 818445
ATOL: 2404
Visa
'H2O Holidays was formed ten years ago and started operations in Lanzarote, Fuerteventura and Tenerife as a specialist tour operator offering quality self-catering holidays at budget prices. Since then the company has grown to include a successful programme in southern Turkey.'
Self-catering holidays: Canary Islands

Haven Europe
Northney Marina, Northney Road, Hayling Island,
Hants PO11 0NH
Admin: 0705 466111
Res: 0705 466111
ABTA: 30627
Visa, Access
Haven offer self-drive cam-

ping and mobile-home holidays in France, Spain and Italy. It is part of The Rank Organisation plc and has been trading for twenty years.
Special interest holidays:
Camping

HF Holidays

Imperial House, Edgware Road, London NW9 5AL
Admin: 081-905 9556
Res: 081-905 9558
Fax: 081-205 0506
ATOL: 710
Visa, Access
'Formed in 1913, HF Holidays is Britain's leading tour operator specializing in special interest and walking holidays. Today, providing active holiday enjoyment for more than 50,000 people every year, the company produces a range of products to suit varying tastes and requirements. Walking holidays are offered in the UK, Europe and in long-haul destinations like New Zealand and the USA. In Spain, holidays are offered in Calpe, Costa Blanca, Barcelona, Puerto de Soller, Majorca and Puerto de la Cruz, Tenerife. Specially trained volunteer leaders conduct the walking holidays, escorting walks and explaining points of interest *en route*.'
Special interest holidays:
Walking and trekking

Holidays for Health

20 Sotheby Road,
London N5 2UR
Admin: 071-359 6690
Res: 071-359 6690
No credit cards accepted
'Holidays for Health offers a variety of holidays in Zahara de los Atunes on the Atlantic coast of Andalucia. It has put together a varied programme of holistic workshops for small groups. Subjects covered include yoga, reflexology, massage and the creative arts. Accommodation is in a small family-run hotel situated right on the beach. Children and non-participating guests are welcome.'
Special interest holidays:
Personal development

Hotels Abroad

5 World's End Lane, Green Street Green,
Orpington BR6 6AA
Admin: 0689 857838
Res: 0689 857838
Fax: 0689 850931
Visa, Access
'At Hotels Abroad we specialize in arranging overnight and short-stay accommodation – mainly for motorists. We've been trading since 1978, and now offer a wider choice of hotels and more locations than any other similar service. Although our main strength is France, Spain is now our second most

important destination. Our service is widely used by travel agents (our biggest client is Going Places) and we arrange *en route* hotels for the clients of over 100 tour operators and P&O Ferries.'
Hotel holidays: All over Spain

Iberotravel
29–31 Elmfield Road,
Bromley, Kent BR11LT
Admin: 081-290 1111
Res: 0532 393020
Fax: 081-313 9808
ABTA: 36746
ATOL: 1368
Visa, Access, Amex
'Sunworld is a brand name of Iberotravel and is an overseas subsidiary of the Grupo Viajes Iberia, a major travel company in Spain. The company's divisions include: Viajes Iberia – a travel agency dealing with business travel, groups and conferences inside and outside Spain; Iberotravel UK, Eurofrance and Iberojet; and the hotel division Iberostar which owns and operates a group of ten hotels and apartments on the islands of Majorca, Gran Canaria and Lanzarote. Sunworld has been operating for three years and in the winter of 1993/94 carried 482,000 passengers. Our destinations include the Balearic Islands, Salou, the Costa Blanca, the Costa del Sol and the Canary Islands.'

Hotel holidays: Balearic Islands, Canary Islands, Andalucia
Self-catering holidays: Balearic Islands

Individual Travellers' Spain
Bignor, Pulborough, West Sussex RH20 1QD
Admin: 07987 461
Res: 07987 485
Fax: 07987 343
ATOL: 2433
AITO
Visa, Access, Amex, Switch
'Launched in 1990 with just a handful of properties in north east Spain, Individual Travellers' Spain is a sister company of Vacances en Campagne – founded in 1976, a leading specialist in self-catering properties throughout France, and Vacanze in Italia – now in its tenth year with properties mainly in Tuscany and Umbria but slowly spreading to other areas of Italy. Our company is aimed at those clients seeking the true Spain, away from the infamous Costas, to those off-the-beaten track areas where the real Spain and its culture exist and thrive. We offer a variety of accommodation from converted farmhouses to apartments and full-blown villas with pools, all at realistic and affordable prices.'

Self-catering holidays:
Andalucia, Catalonia, Castile and Leon, Valencia, Balearic Islands

Inghams
10 Putney Hill,
London SW15 6AX
Admin: 081-789 6555
Res: 081-780 0909
Fax: 081-785 2045
ABTA: 36750
ATOL: 25
Visa, Access
'Inghams is celebrating its sixtieth birthday this year. Originally a winter sports company and now the second largest, it also offers a summer Lakes and Mountains programme, holidays in the Indian Ocean and European city breaks, featuring thirty-seven cities. Inghams is owned by Hotelplan which itself is a subsidiary of the Swiss Migros Corporation. Spanish cities included in the Eurobreak programme include Barcelona, Madrid and Seville. The arrangements are ideal for the independent traveller and allow complete flexibility of choice, including duration and choice of travel by air, rail, coach or car. There are direct scheduled flights from up to nineteen UK airports to the most popular destinations. The hotels are carefully chosen to give a range of prices and all are in the city centres. All rooms have private facilities. Breakfast is always included.'
Special interest holidays: City breaks

Insight Holidays
6 Gareloch Road, Port Glasgow PA14 5XH
Admin: 0475 742366
Res: 0800 393 393
Fax: 0475 742073
ABTA: 18254
ATOL: 1513
AITO
Visa, Access
Insight offer escorted coach touring holidays all over Europe. 'We'll show you the sights you always wanted to see as well as others you never knew existed. You'll meet and mingle with people, share their history, art and culture – and sample their cuisine. Our itineraries provide two- and three-night stops so you have the time to do the things you want and we stay in hotels which are mostly first-class or better, well located in the cities and close to major scenic attractions.'
Special interest holidays: Coach holidays

Inspirations Holidays
Saxley Court, Horley,
Surrey RH6 7AS
Admin: 0293 820207
Res: 0293 822244
Fax: 0293 821732

ABTA: 6374
ATOL: 2314
Visa, Access, Switch
Inspirations offers hotel and self-catering beach holidays on the islands of Tenerife, Gran Canaria and Lanzarote.
Hotel holidays: Canary Islands
Self-catering holidays: Canary Islands

Interhome
383 Richmond Road, Twickenham TW1 2EF
Admin: 081-891 1294
Res: 081-891 1294
Fax: 081-891 5331
ABTA: 3684
Visa, Access
'Interhome has been letting out holiday homes since 1965. It is part of the Swiss Hotelplan Group. Over the years it has built up a large selection of privately owned houses and apartments for rent throughout Europe. At the last count it was offering a choice of over 20,000 proper- ties of all sizes and price ranges.'

Islands in the Sun
31 Star Street, Ware, Herts SG12 7AA
Admin: 0920 484515
Res: 0920 484515
Fax: 0920 484006
ATOL: 2751
Visa, Access
'Islands in the Sun is a small family-run business, offering a personal service for people looking for a good-quality self-catering holiday in either Lanzarote or Fuerteventura in the Canary Islands. It offers a range of accommodation, much privately owned: villas with and without pools; apartments in small and large complexes; beach and seafront locations; some properties close to resort amenities and some offering near-solitude.'
Self-catering holidays: Canary Islands

James Villa Holidays
The Coach House, 95 High Street, West Malling, Kent ME19 6NA
Admin: 0732 840846
Res: 0732 840846
Fax: 0732 872092
ATOL: 2730
Visa, Access
'James Villa Holidays is a fully-bonded tour operator and has been established since 1984. The company offers self-catering holidays to the Canary Islands. All the villas have been personally inspected by the staff who are able to give detailed informa- tion about the accom- modation and the resort.'
Self-catering holidays: Canary Islands

Kirker Holidays
3 New Concordia Wharf, Mill Street, London SE1 2BB
Admin: 071-231 3333
Res: 071-231 3333
Fax: 071-231 4771
ABTA: 38012
ATOL: 2450
AITO
Visa, Access, Amex, Switch
Founded in 1986, Kirker is an independent company specializing in short breaks to European cities, taking around 15,000 people abroad each year.
Hotel holidays: Andalucia
Special interest holidays: City breaks

Lanzarote Leisure
4 Lytton Road, New Barnet, Hertfordshire EN5 5BY
Admin: 081-449 7441
Res: 081-449 7441
Fax: 081-440 6383
ATOL: 2157
AITO
Visa, Access
'We have specialized for over thirteen years in letting villas and apartments in the Canary Islands. The properties featured in our brochure, most of which are privately owned, are furnished to a high standard and many are situated within a short distance of beautiful beaches. Our staff are familiar with all resorts and properties and can therefore assist you in choosing accommodation most suitable for your requirements. We offer holidays to Lanzarote, Fuerteventura and Tenerife.'
Self-catering holidays: Canary Islands

Longshot Golf Holidays
Meon House, College Street, Petersfield GU32 3JN
Admin: 0730 266561
Res: 0730 268621
Fax: 0730 231998
ABTA: 43788
ATOL: 016
AITO
Visa, Access, Amex, Diners
'Longshot Golf Holidays has been operating for twenty-one years and is a division of Meon Travel – a successful family business, established in 1964. We offer quality hotels and resorts suitable for golfers and their families – all offering generous child and group discounts. Golf arrangements can be made with a guaranteed tee-time reservation service with free or discounted green fees or we can offer competitive holiday golf during one of our Amateur Gala Tournament weeks. Travel arrangements can be made from London and regional airports with flexible duration holidays tailored to your exact requirements. Car hire and the services of the Longshot golf

resort representative are auto-matically included.'
Special interest holidays:
Golfing holidays

Longwood Holidays
182 Longwood Gardens,
Ilford, Essex IG5 0EW
Admin: 081-551 9988
Res: 081-551 4494
Fax: 081-551 7891
ABTA: 41636
ATOL: 2199
Visa, Access, Amex
'Having been trading for the last ten years, we have built up an excellent working relationship with the Spanish hotels. We use the services of the scheduled airline Viva Air (a subsidiary of Iberia), allowing us to offer holidays of various durations. Flexibility plays a large part in our service. We feature Marbella, Banalmadena, Fuengirola and Torremolinos and offer a wide-ranging choice of hotels.'
Hotel holidays: Andalucia
Self-catering holidays:
Andalucia
Special interest holidays:
Golfing holidays

Made to Measure Holidays
43 East Street,
Chichester PO19 1HX
Admin: 0243 533333
Res: 0243 533333
Fax: 0243 778431
ABTA: 91921

ATOL: 1006
Visa, Access
'Made to Measure Holidays has been established for twenty years and is still a totally independent, family-owned company. Each year it carries 3000 customers abroad. It specializes in custom-made itineraries to exclusive hotels. Made to Measure's brochure entitled 'Romantic Escapes' captivates the imagination of people with a particular celebration in mind – maybe a wedding anniversary or a special birth-day, or even a honeymoon. The hotels have been chosen for their combination of the five Cs: charm, character, calm, courtesy and cuisine.'
Special interest holidays: City breaks

Magic of Spain
227 Shepherds Bush Road,
London W6 7AS
Admin: 081-748 4999
Res: 081-748 7575
Fax: 081-563 0480
ABTA: 97275
ATOL: 2398
AITO
Visa, Access, Amex
'Magic of Spain is part of the Air Travel Group, which in turn is part of Granada plc, the UK's fiftieth largest company. Founded in 1989, it will carry more than 15,000 passengers to Spain in 1994

and is now firmly established as a leading tour operator to Spain. It offers an enormous variety of holidays all over mainland Spain and Majorca in both hotels and self-catering properties. Magic of Spain appeals not only to the art and culture enthusiasts, but also to people looking for a traditional beach holiday in Spain's finest resorts. Its range of holidays stretches from 'Pick and Mix' holidays (where you can tailormake your own itinerary) in Andalucia, Catalonia, Castile and Green Spain to luxury villas and quality hotels in the unspoilt and attractive areas of the coast. It also offers the famous Paradors and a wide selection of character hotels in enchanting locations. It aims to give a selection of the most interesting accommodation available in Spain, be it a converted watermill, an old ducal palace or simply an outstanding view.'
Hotel holidays: Andalucia, Cantabria/Asturias, Catalonia, Balearic Islands, Castile and Leon, Valencia
Self-catering holidays: Andalucia, Balearic Islands, Catalonia, Valencia

Majorca Farmhouse Holidays

Hunters Cottage, Row Lane, Dunsden, Reading RG4 9PS

Admin: 0734 462181
Res: 0734 462181
Fax: 0734 461362
'Majorca Farmhouse Holidays offers luxurious farmhouses, country homes, apartments, posadas and hotels in the areas of Puerto Pollensa, Cala San Vincente and Cala D'or. Eighty per cent of customers return the following year.'
Hotel holidays: Balearic Islands
Self-catering holidays: Balearic Islands

Martin Randall Travel

10 Barley Mow Passage, Chiswick, London W4 4PH
Admin: 081-742 3355
Res: 081-742 3355
Fax: 081-742 1066
ABTA: 16070
ATOL: 1585
AITO
Visa, Access
'Martin Randall Travel is a leading company in the field of art and music tours. Set up in 1988, we carry 1500 people annually to destinations throughout West and Eastern Europe, the Middle East and North Africa. Our programme of Spanish tours this year includes Madrid and Toledo, Art in Madrid, The Road to Santiago, Granada and Cordoba, Andalucia, Castile and the Pyrenees. The particular feature of our tours is that they are led by a specialist who is an expert in the culture

of the area. The tours follow an intensive itinerary of cultural visits, studying Spanish art, architecture and history. The lecturer, who is usually an art historian, talks on site to the group about the venues being visited. The groups are limited to between twenty and twenty-five participants, in order to promote social cohesion and to ensure that everyone is within easy earshot of the lecturer. Our tours to Spain usually operate in spring or autumn (March/April and September/October), as the temperatures are best then for itineraries which involve quite a lot of walking and sometimes a number of hotel changes. However, we have recently introduced a Christmas tour to Granada and Cordoba. Our clientele tends to belong to the more mature age bracket and includes many individuals who enjoy travelling with others of similar interests.'
Special interest holidays: Art history tours

Meon Villa Holidays
Meon House, Petersfield,
Hants GU32 3JN
Admin: 0730 266561
Res: 0730 268411
Fax: 0730 268482
ABTA: 43788
ATOL: 16

AITO
Visa, Access, Amex
'Meon Villas has been operating since 1967 offering independent villas with private pools in a wide range of destinations. Meon Villas is the main programme of the Meon Group of Companies, who carry around 30,000 passengers annually on a range of specialist holidays. Meon offer around 180 villas in Spain, all of which are individual, privately owned properties with a private swimming pool. The areas of Spain featured are the Costa del Sol and the Costa Blanca, the islands of Majorca, Minorca and Ibiza, as well as Lanzarote in the Canaries. All holidays are inclusive of flights from Gatwick, car hire, maid service, a welcome food pack and the assistance of Meon's experienced local representatives. Flights are also available from a selection of regional airports.'
Self-catering holidays:
Andalucia, Valencia, Balearic Islands, Canary Islands

Minorca Sailing Holidays
58 Kew Road, Richmond,
Surrey TW9 2PQ
Admin: 081-948 2106
Res: 081-948 2106
Fax: 081-332 6528
ATOL: 1248
AITO

Visa, Access
'Minorca Sailing Holidays is a small, independently run company which has been in operation for over twenty years. The emphasis is on flexibility and having fun, while you learn to sail or improve your skills. Fully qualified RYA instructors are on hand to give tuition or a guiding hand, whichever is required, while you enjoy the range of dinghies and wind-surfers carefully chosen to appeal to all abilities. Families, couples and individuals are all welcomed at the sailing centre and all can be fully confident that their needs will be catered for. Approximately 1500 people each year enjoy our holidays and many come back year after year. Accommodation includes a hotel with pool, private villas with their own pool and self-catering apartments. Crèche facilities and a nanny service are offered.'
Special interest holidays:
Sailing, Windsurfing

Mundi Color Holidays
276 Vauxhall Bridge Road,
London SW1V 1BE
Admin: 071-828 6021
Res: 071-828 6021
Fax: 071-834 5752
ABTA: 46292
ATOL: 799
AITO

Visa, Access, Amex, Diners
'Mundi Color, founded in 1969, is a sister company of Iberia Airlines and arranges travel for nearly one million visitors to Spain each year. Mundi Color can tailor-make itineraries with a choice of over 2000 properties throughout Spain, including the famous Paradors. In addition to resorts such as the Canary Islands and Majorca, Mundi Color features city breaks, tours through less well-known regions, gastronomy tours and luxury travel aboard the Al Andalus Express train. The company features only scheduled flights with Iberia, Viva Air and Aviaco, but for clients who do not wish to fly, it also works closely with P&O and Brittany Ferries to offer direct access to northern Spain. The Hotel Color flexible voucher scheme offers up to 50 per cent savings to independent travellers. The scheme also allows clients to book Avis car hire at a fraction of the normal cost.'
Hotel holidays: All over Spain
Self-catering holidays: All over Spain
Special interest holidays: City breaks, Paradors and pousadas, Coach holidays, Fly-drive, Train holidays

Owners Abroad Travel
2nd Floor, Astral Towers,
Betts Way, Crawley,
West Sussex RH10 2GX
Admin: 0293 554466
Res: 0293 554455
ATOL: 2600
Visa, Access
Tjaereborg, Martin Rooks,
Sunfare and Timsway form
the direct-sell arm of the
Owners Abroad Group. They
carry approximately 350,000
clients annually.

PCI Holidays
137a South Road, Haywards
Heath, West Sussex RH16 4LY
Admin: 0444 440606
Res: 0444 440606
Fax: 0444 440999
ATOL: 3318
Visa, Access, Amex
'The company Property Care
International was formed in
1989 to manage and let properties of the highest quality in
Catalonia and Minorca. We
have a wide selection of
apartments, villas, cottages,
town houses and farmhouses.
All are maintained locally by
our own staff and family. This
year we have launched PCI
Motoring Holidays, specifi-
cally aimed at those wishing
to drive to Catalonia with
stops in France – or even holidays in France. Our Golf
Holidays continue to grow
and can be adapted to suit
groups or individuals,

offering access to six chal-
lenging courses, each with
stunning scenery and excep-
tionally good value in the low
and mid seasons.'
Hotel holidays: Catalonia
Self-catering holidays:
Catalonia, Balearic Islands
Special interest holidays:
Golfing holidays

Page & Moy
136–140 London Road,
Leicester LE2 1EN
Admin: 0533 542000
Res: 0533 524433
Fax: 0533 524124
ABTA: 47026
ATOL: 133
Visa, Access
Page & Moy has been oper-
ating for over thirty years
and was one of the founder
members of ABTA.
Hotel holidays: All over Spain
Special interest holidays:
Cooking holidays

Palmer & Parker Holidays
The Beacon, Penn,
Buckinghamshire HP10 8ND
Admin: 0494 815411
Res: 0494 815411
Fax: 0494 814184
ABTA: 47134
ATOL: 164
'Palmer & Parker villa holi-
days has for twenty-two years
specialized in exceptionally
comfortable villas at substan-
tial rentals – £1000 to £5000
weekly, dependent on size

and season. All holidays include a minimum of two cars.'
Self-catering holidays:
Andalucia

Panorama Holiday Group
29 Queen's Road, Brighton, Sussex BN1 3YN
Admin: 0273 202391
Res: 0273 206531
Fax: 0273 205338
ABTA: 65448
ATOL: 0782
AITO
Visa, Access, Amex
'It is now forty years since the original Panorama was started by the Hayes Family. Since 1954 the company has continued to grow and has become one of the major independent tour operators. The company first introduced holidays to Majorca in 1957 and to Ibiza in 1966. The Hayes Family has continued to live and work in Ibiza in Es Cana, running the Zodiac complex of apartments, shops and restaurants.'
Hotel holidays: Balearic Islands
Self-catering holidays: Balearic Islands

Patricia Wildblood
Calne, Wiltshire SN11 0LP
Admin: 0249 817023
Res: 081-658 6722
Fax: 0249 813976
ABTA: 63194
ATOL: 1276
Visa, Access
'Patricia Wildblood has been organizing self-catering holidays on the island of Minorca for twenty-three years. The company offers villas and apartments by the sea or old Minorcan houses in the countryside. Flights are from Gatwick, Manchester and Newcastle with other departure airports available on request. The company also operates holidays to Tuscany, the Algarve and Tunisia.'
Self-catering holidays: Balearic Islands

Portland Holidays
218 Great Portland Street, London W1N 5HG
Admin: 071-380 0281
Res: 071-388 5111
Fax: 071-387 1269
ABTA: 5217
ATOL: 2524
Visa, Access, Switch
'Portland Holidays was set up in 1979 as a sister company of Thomson Holidays to sell holidays directly to the public. We presently carry 200,000 passengers annually. By booking direct clients save the cost of the agent's commission which is usually around 10 per cent of the price of the holiday. Our team of reservations advisers have personal knowledge of all resorts and accommodation featured in the Portland brochure. We

have a well-established programme to the Costa de Almeria and the Costa Blanca both in summer and winter.'
Hotel holidays: Andalucia, Balearics, Canary Islands, Valencia
Self-catering holidays: All over Spain, Andalucia

Prestige Holidays
14 Market Place, Ringwood, Hants BH24 1JA
Admin: 0425 480400
Res: 0425 480400
Fax: 0425 470139
ABTA: 2265
ATOL: 2509
AITO
Visa, Access, Amex, Diners
'All our realistically priced hotels and apartments are well known to us and we offer advice with pleasure. We prefer, wherever possible, to use scheduled flights for our clients – they offer protection against charter delays. Prestige holidays can be individually tailored to suit business commitments or a budget. We have over 100 years of experience as a management team.'
Hotel holidays: Canary Islands
Self-catering holidays: Canary Islands

Prima Villas
Brunswick House, Harbour Avenue, Plymouth PL4 0BN
Admin: 0752 256678
Res: 0752 256678
Fax: 0752 251699
AITO
Visa, Access, Amex, Switch
'Prima Villas offers a range of villas in Catalonia and the Costa Blanca. The range has been continually refined over a number of years with most properties having a private pool but representing value for money. We have helpful agency staff in Catalonia and resident English agents on the Costa Blanca who can arrange airport pick-ups and starter hampers. Prima Villas, part of the Kingsland Holidays Group, was established in 1987.'
Self-catering holidays: Catalonia, Valencia

Prospect Music & Art Tours
454–458 Chiswick High Road, London W4 5TT
Admin: 081-995 2163
Res: 081-995 2151
Fax: 081-742 1969
ATOL: 2719
Visa, Access
'Prospect Music and Art Tours has been organizing cultural holidays for over ten years. We offer four products: fully guided art tours, in Spain these include Andalucia Cities of the Reconquista and Spanish painting in Madrid; cultural weekends with Madrid and Barcelona as popular destinations; art tours to places further afield than

Europe, for example, Tunisia, Syria or Jordan; and opera and music holidays. All our tours use scheduled flights and we stay in comfortable and convenient hotels. No group is ever larger than twenty and is often between ten and fifteen.'
Special interest holidays: Art history tours, Music holidays

Ramblers Holidays
Box 43,
Welwyn Garden AL8 6PQ
Admin: 0707 331133
Res: 0707 331133
Fax: 0707 333276
ABTA: 50940
ATOL: 990
AITO
Visa, Access
'Ramblers Holidays was established in 1946. It now carries around 12,000 passengers per year. All Ramblers holidays are graded and vary in length from one week to three. Parties generally consist of between sixteen and twenty people. Besides holidays for walkers, from tough to easy, we offer a range of tours for nature lovers, photographers and those wishing to improve their Spanish, and interesting sightseeing trips nearly always including some easy walking. In Spain, destinations include Alpujarras, Andalucia, Majorca, Minorca, the Pyrenees, the Picos de Europa, the Valley of Jerte and the Sierra de Gredos in central Spain. Ramblers holidays are unsuitable for children under sixteen years of age.'
Special interest holidays:
Walking and trekking

Rosemary & Frances Villas
Time Off, Chester Close,
London SW1X 7BQ
Admin: 071-235 8825
Res: 071-235 8825
Fax: 071-259 6093
ABTA: 58374
ATOL: 2315
AITO
Visa, Access
'Rosemary and Frances Villas is a division of Time Off (the city break tour operator) and specializes in the rental of villas and apartments with swimming pools. Our properties are situated in Andalucia, Tuscany, Umbria and the Amalfi coast. Most of our properties have been visited by us and have been chosen for their quality and/or location. We offer privately owned properties and though our brochure only shows a small selection of villas and apartments we have a portfolio of over 300 houses. We specialize in 'tailormaking' holidays for those who prefer to stay in quieter places – those for whom a private villa with its own pool has more appeal than a hotel in a busy

beach resort. Each booking is handled on a personal basis and using our detailed knowledge of Spanish villas we take care to make sure our clients book the property that best suits their varied needs.'
Self-catering holidays: Andalucia

Secret Spain
Model Farm, Hightown Green, Rattlesden, Bury St Edmunds, Suffolk IP30 0SY
Admin: 0449 737664
Res: 0449 737664
Fax: 0449 737850
AITO
Visa, Access, Amex
'A small, specialist company which seeks out the undiscovered charms of hidden Spain. Established for over six years, Secret Spain is a sister company to La France des Villages. It is fully-bonded and sends around 2000 people abroad annually. It features a programme of self-drive holidays, particularly to north/north-west Spain – Asturias and Galicia. In Asturias it offers a selection of traditional houses for self-catering, both in the mountains and on or near the coast. It also offers some small, family-run hotels. New for 1994 are riding holidays in the Picos de Europa mountains. In Galicia self-catering houses and small hotels are featured, also bed and breakfast accommoda-

tion in Manor houses in the hills inland. Two-centre holidays incorporating northern Portugal are possible. In Pollensa in northern Majorca converted farmhouses with private pools are offered.'
Hotel holidays: Cantabria/Asturias, Galicia
Self-catering holidays: Cantabria/Asturias, Galicia, Balearic Islands
Special interest holidays: Horseriding, Walking and trekking, Angling

Sherpa Expeditions
131a Heston Road, Hounslow, Middlesex TW5 0RD
Admin: 081-577 2717
Res: 081-577 2717
Fax: 081-572 9788
ATOL: 1185
Visa, Access
'Sherpa is a company dedicated to walkers and walking holidays. It has been operating for over twenty years and carries around 3000 people annually. It offers specialist walking holidays for all grades of walks to unknown Spain – destinations include the Picos de Europa, the Sierra Nevada and Majorca. The walks are carefully researched and led by expert guides. Accommodation is in village pensions and tavernas. Baggage is transported.'
Special interest holidays:
Walking and trekking

Sovereign

Astral Towers, Betts Way,
Crawley,
West Sussex RH10 2GX
Admin: 0293 599988
Res: 0293 599988
Fax: 0293 588322
ABTA: 68342
ATOL: 230
Visa, Access
'Sovereign is part of the Owners Abroad Group and has been established for twenty-three years.'
Hotel holidays: All over Spain

Spanish Affair

George House, 5/7 Humbolt Road, London W6 8QH
Admin: 071-385 8127
Res: 071-385 8127
Fax: 071-381 5423
ATOL: 2334
'Spanish Affair is a trading division of French Affair Limited which started operating in 1986 and offers self-catering and hotel holidays to France. Spanish Affair features country properties in Andalucia.'
Self-catering holidays: Andalucia

Spanish Harbour Holidays

The Cottage, Upper Street,
Dyrham, Chippenham,
Wilts SN14 8HN
Admin: 0272 373759
Res: 0272 373759
Fax: 0272 373571
ATOL: 3152
AITO
Visa, Access
'Founded in 1985, Spanish Harbour Holidays is a privately owned company. We specialize in providing holidays to the unspoilt coastal and mountain villages of Catalonia. Our holidays are tailormade to fit individual requirements. Our staff are all familiar with the villages and properties and with a customer base of only just 2000 can guarantee clients a personal and caring service. Our properties range from simple one-bedroom apartments overlooking the beach to luxury villas with pools – all are personally selected and frequently inspected. Our hotel holidays are based on family-run hotels.'
Hotel holidays: Catalonia
Self-catering holidays: Catalonia

Spantrek

79 Egmont Street, Mossley,
Ashton-U-Lyme,
Lancashire OL5 9NF
Admin: 0457 836250
Res: 0457 836250
ATOL: 3232
Visa, Access, Diners, Switch
'Spantrek, now in its ninth year of operation, is an independent, fully-bonded travel company, specializing in high-quality rambling, high-level trekking and wildlife holidays in the unspoilt mountain

regions of Spain. Our main venue is the Picos de Europa mountains in northern Spain where we are based for much of the season from April to October. We carry around 140 clients annually. Spantrek places great emphasis on the real Spain with ties in the community. This is imperative in the Picos since local culture and traditions are very strong – consequently our visitors do feel part of the community. Since we are a small company, we are often able to provide the individual attention which is so often lacking in larger organizations. Our attention to detail and emphasis on the client's enjoyment have resulted in many satisfied customers and re-bookings. Although our main base is in the Picos de Europa (walks, rambles, high-level treks and wildlife), we also operate holidays in the Pyrenees (ornithology), Sierra de Gredos in mid Spain (walks and rambles), Tenerife (wildlife), Sierra de Grazalema in Andalucia (walking and wildlife), and the Douro Valley and the Algarve in Portugal. In addition we have planned winter breaks for 1994/95 to the Picos as well as a completely new programme for the Spring into South America under the company name of Terranova Tours. This will encompass countries such as Mexico, Bolivia, Argentina, Ecuador and Brazil.'

Self-catering holidays:
Cantabria/Asturias
Special interest holidays:
Walking and trekking, Natural history

Speedwing
26 Temple Fortune Parade, London NW11 0QS
Admin: 081-998 8157
Res: 081-905 5252
Fax: 081-458 3234
ABTA: 8153
ATOL: 2546
AITO
Visa, Access
'Speedwing 1994 Villas with Pools programme features luxury villas with private pools in the Costa Blanca, Majorca, Minorca, Ibiza, Lanzarote and Florida. The Villas with Pools programme has been in operation for five years and carries 5000 passengers a year. Speedwing also trades under the name of IHS Travel which includes All Abroad. We offer complete privacy and seclusion to clients who want to get away from it all. We also offer a free Group B hire car in the cost of the holiday. Villas range from two to four bedrooms, all providing a private garden with swimming pool, fully-fitted kitchen, lounge/dining

area, fitted bedrooms and bathrooms. Some villas also offer patios with barbecues, verandahs, TV and satellite, some offer maid service. Many villas are second homes, therefore clients can be assured of staying in beautifully presented properties.'
Self-catering holidays: Valencia, Balearic Islands

Style Holidays
Coomb House, 7 St Johns Road, Isleworth, Middlesex TW7 6NA
Admin: 081-568 1999
Res: 081-568 1999
Fax: 081-758 1032
ABTA: 6374
ATOL: 2314
Visa, Access
'Style Holidays has been operating for two years and during that time has built up a loyal group of repeat customers. It offers private villas with pools and apartments on the island of Minorca. Child discounts and free places are offered. One child aged over two and under sixteen travelling and sharing an apartment with two or more adults can travel free on certain specified dates. At selected properties car hire is included in the holiday price.'
Self-catering holidays: Balearic Islands

Sunsites
Canute Court, Toft Road, Knutsford WA16 0NL
Admin: 0565 625549
Res: 0565 625555
Fax: 0565 652874
ABTA: 56449
AITO
Visa, Access
'Sunsites is a specialist self-drive luxury camping and mobile-home tour operator based in Knutsford, Cheshire. The company is a subsidiary of Eurocamp plc, the market leader in this sector. The Eurocamp Group has traded profitably for twenty-one years and its shares are listed on the London Stock Market. Sunsites is a member of ABTA and AITO and carries in excess of 40,000 holiday-makers annually. The Sunsites 1994 Summer Value brochure features the top category Camping Cypsela which is located near Playa de Pals on the Costa Brava. Our holidays are very flexible, with no fixed departure dates or length of stay, customers can tailor their itinerary to suit their own needs. As well as luxury accommodation on a wide range of well-equipped sites, the additional benefits of the Sunsites Courier and Children's Courier service, the comprehensive Travel Pack and the children's funpacks ensure that cus-

tomers get the most out of their Sunsites holiday.'
Special interest holidays: Camping, Caravans and mobile homes

Swan Hellenic
77 New Oxford Street, London WC1A 1PP
Admin: 071-831 1515
Res: 071-831 1515
ATOL: 307
Swan Hellenic has been operating cultural cruises for forty years. 'The 1994 programme comprises eighteen different themed cruises around the Mediterranean. Our cruising experience is far more than a relaxing way to travel to some of the more interesting places in the Western world. It's about absorbing atmospheres of both yesteryear and today and breathing life into aspects of history most of us vaguely remember but perhaps never truly understood. Our itineraries are mostly of two weeks' duration but during the summer there are two one-week cruises which can also be linked with adjacent itineraries to form two-, three- or four-week holidays. All our journeys are value for money with no annoying hidden extras, for all main excursions, together with some alternative trips, are included in the fare and there is a no-tipping policy on board.'

Special interest holidays: Art history, Cruises

Tall Stories
67a High Street, Walton on Thames, Surrey KT12 1BR
Admin: 0932 252002
Res: 0932 252002
Fax: 0932 225145
'Tall Stories was formed in 1991 to give clients an alternative to "on the beach holidays". The company offers adventure holidays in Austria, France and Spain. In each country it features a holiday which is designed to let the client experience a different sport each day: coastal exploration; diving; mountain biking; water skiing; sailing or trekking. Each sport is guided by experts using first-class equipment. In Spain the holidays are based on the Catalan coast in the village of L'Estartit and the accommodation is in the Hotel Santa Anna.'
Special interest holidays: Adventure holidays

The Travel Club of Upminster
Station Road, Upminster RM14 2TT
Admin: 0708 223000
Res: 0708 225000
Fax: 0708 229678
ABTA: 59165
ATOL: 172
AITO

Visa, Access

'The Travel Club of Upminster has been in business for over fifty years. It was started as a family business for family holidays and is still owned and run by Rene and Paul, wife and son of the founder Harry Chandler. The company believes that small is beautiful and has never struggled to increase numbers at the expense of the personal touch. It carries around 20,000 passengers a year, about half to the islands of Majorca and Minorca. The company has sent holidaymakers to Puerto Pollensa on Majorca since 1958. It offers a complete range of self-catering and hotel accommodation, from luxury villas to simple beachside hostels. The Travel Club of Upminster is not a club – anyone can join, but its holidays cannot be bought through travel agents and so it enjoys a high level of loyalty from its customers, many of whom return year after year. Its speciality is a personal level of service that cannot be matched by larger companies.'

Hotel holidays: Balearic Islands
Self-catering holidays: Balearic Islands
Special interest holidays: Birdwatching, Golfing holidays, Natural history, Archaeology

The Villa Club

154–156 Victoria Road,
Cambridge CB4 3DZ
Admin: 0223 311322
Res: 0223 311322
Fax: 0223 314423
ABTA: 99694
ATOL: 2270
AITO
Visa, Access, Amex

'The Villa Club, based in Cambridge, has a portfolio of self-catering accommodation including top-quality villas with private swimming pools, small exclusive developments of villas and bungalows with shared pools, and beachfront apartments. It is run by the privately owned tour operator European Villas who carried around 15,000 people in 1993 and who have over ten years' experience in the industry. The Villa Club programme also covers the Algarve, France, Turkey, Corfu, Gozo and Tuscany, but Spain offers the largest choice of properties, covering the Costa Blanca, Costa Brava, Ibiza, Majorca and Minorca. All properties are contracted personally by the Directors, with a view to both interior quality and comfort, location, peacefulness, views, access to facilities and suitability for families. The holidays are all offered on a rental-only basis or inclusive of flights from over ten UK airports, with

child discounts on all dates, and unlimited free child places available. Additional services include car hire, welcome food packs, maid service, video and TV hire, cots, highchairs, playpens, coolbags etc. The emphasis is on quality and personal service, with full resort assistance if necessary. Clients can book direct, or through independent travel agents.'
Self-catering holidays: Balearic Islands, Valencia, Catalonia

Thomson Holidays
Greater London House,
Hampstead Road,
London NW1 7SD
Admin: 071-387 9321
Res: 021 632 6282
ABTA: 5217
ATOL: 2524
Visa, Access, Switch
'Thomson has organized holidays since the early 1970s. Part of the Canadian-owned Thomson Corporation, it has the financial backing and security of a large well-known company. As the UK's largest tour operator Thomson carries four million people annually. Spain accounts for over a third of operations and Thomson is renowned as the market leader in this area. Thomson has developed a range of holidays to suit many tastes. With the family market in mind from the beginning,

Thomson has offered childcare. The Baby Patrollers of the 1970s gave way to the Big T children's clubs in 1977 which have grown in number and expertise. In the summer of 1994 over 100 Big T Clubs were in operation offering daytime and evening activities for four to eleven year olds. Many supervisors are qualified nursery nurses. Holidays are featured in Summer Sun, Winter Sun, Skytours, Horizon and Villas and Apartments brochures, with more specialized hotels featured in A La Carte, Small and Friendly and CityBreaks brochures.'
Hotel holidays: All over Spain
Self-catering holidays: All over Spain
Special interest holidays: City breaks

Travellers' Way
Hewell Lane, Tardebigge,
Bromsgrove,
Worcestershire B60 1LP
Admin: 0527 836377
Res: 0527 836791
Fax: 0527 836159
ABTA: 5180
ATOL: 2709
Visa, Access
'Travellers' Way offers self-catering and hotel holidays to "unspoilt Spain". Throughout our brochure you will find mountain villages which have changed little over the years,

undiscovered coastal areas with uncrowded beaches, traditional fishing villages and fabulous cities. Our self-catering accommodation ranges from simple village houses to luxury villas with private pools. Our hotels range from comfortable, little, family-run establishments to luxurious four- and five-star hotels and Paradors which are typical of the region in which they are situated. Our coastal hotels are located away from the busy resorts and the city hotels are conveniently located. Touring holidays are also featured and can be combined with a week in one of our self-catering houses. Most of our complete holidays are based around scheduled flights.'
Hotel holidays: Andalucia, Galicia, Cantabria/Asturias
Self-catering holidays: Andalucia, Valencia, Galicia, Cantabria/Asturias, Pyrenees
Special interest holidays: City breaks, Paradors and pousadas

Ultimate Holidays
Ultimate House, Twyford Business Centre, London Road, Bishop's Stortford CM23 3YT
Admin: 0279 657776
Res: 0279 755527
Fax: 0279 655603
ABTA: 7841

ATOL: 2676
AITO
Visa, Access
'Ultimate Holidays has been trading for five years and has a wide range of products including city breaks, skiing, summer and winter sun holidays, long-haul and seat-only deals. It features Majorca, Minorca, Tenerife, Lanzarote, Ibiza, Costa del Sol, Madrid, Barcelona and Murcia. As a medium-sized tour operator, Ultimate can offer a highly flexible service and can arrange everything from a fully-inclusive long-haul holiday in Singapore to one day's car hire in Spain.'
Hotel holidays: Balearic Islands, Canary Islands, Andalucia
Self-catering holidays: Balearic Islands, Canary Islands, Andalucia
Special interest holidays: City breaks

Unicorn Holidays
2 Place Farm, Wheathampstead, Herts AL4 8SB
Admin: 0582 83 4400
Res: 0582 83 4400
Fax: 0582 83 1133
ABTA: 99798
ATOL: 2431
AITO
Visa, Access
'Unicorn Holidays, now in its sixth year, specializes in

tailormade holidays featuring the Paradors and other excellent hotels. Paradors are hotels, many of which are converted from historic castles, palaces, monasteries etc, which are situated throughout the whole of Spain. Unicorn Holidays publishes the only brochure in the UK which has a description and a picture of each Parador. Not all Paradors are of the same standard, therefore any itinerary needs careful planning to discover the best of Spain. This takes time and first-hand knowledge, which is what Unicorn offers to its clients. To help in the planning of clients' holidays, we have suggested itineraries in our brochure but they are only suggestions and can, and usually are, amended. Travel is by scheduled airlines on a fly drive basis or "take your own car'"via the ferry routes to northern Spain. Our holidays are for those who wish to escape the mass market. They are for people who take an interest in the real Spain, through which they are travelling, and who require comfort and civilized surroundings while discovering the delights of inland Spain.'

Special interest holidays:
Paradors and pousadas

Velo Vacances
20b Heol-y-Brenin,
Caerfyrddin, Dyfed SA31 1BH
Admin: 0267 221182
Res: 0267 221182
No credit cards accepted
'Velo Vacances has been organizing cycling holidays for five years – catering for the interests of both novice and experienced cyclists. It arranges transport from the UK to the holiday destination, provides quality bikes, detailed route maps and guides, books friendly hotels with good food, transports luggage and provides full mechanical back-up. It is possible to cycle as a group or individually, making personal decisions regarding routes, distances, sight-seeing and lunch stops. Staying two nights in most of the hotels gives the client the freedom to follow his own interests in the locality. The length of the holidays varies from eight days at Easter and Whitsun, to eleven and twelve days during the summer months. Group sizes are limited to a maximum of sixteen cyclists. In addition this year in Spain the company are offering two activity holidays combining social events with cycling, a guided off-road holiday into Navarra and independent camping holidays. The company also offers holidays to France.'

Special interest holidays:
Cycling holidays

Villa Select
Arden Court, Arden Road,
Alcester,
Warwickshire B49 6HN
Admin: 0789 764909
Res: 0789 764909
Fax: 0789 400355
Visa, Access
'Villa Select has been operating for eleven years. The
company has an impressive
following of return clients,
these represent over 40 per
cent of its annual turnover.
All of the company's villas are
privately owned and are
therefore unique within their
particular resort. It believes
that villa holidays should
offer privacy and freedom
and strive to achieve that. The
service offered is based on the
rental of a private villa, inclusive of maid service on a per-
week basis. This means that as
long as the maximum occu-
pancy of the villa is not
exceeded, the cost of the villa
remains the same however
many persons share the property. Aircraft seats can be
purchased through the
company and are treated
separately.'
Self-catering holidays: Balearic
Islands, Canary Islands

Villanza
429 Springfield Road,
Chelmsford, Essex CM2 6AP
Admin: 0245 262496
Res: 0245 262496
Fax: 0245 359507
ATOL: 2169
Visa, Access
'Villanza offers villa and
apartment holidays on the
islands of Lanzarote and
Fuerteventura in the Canary
Islands.'
Self-catering holidays: Canary
Islands

Vintage Spain
75 Rampton Road,
Willingham,
Cambridge CB4 5JQ
Admin: 0954 261431
Res: 0954 261431
Fax: 0954 260819
ABTA: 4281
ATOL: 2787
AITO
Visa, Access, Switch
'Vintage Spain has been operating for five years and is
a small, country-house
specialist, carrying some 2000
passengers annually. Its
working directors each have
over twenty years' experience
in travel and the company
ethos is strictly one of a very
personal, honest and flexible
service. It ensures that clients
book a holiday tailormade to
their needs, that will not
disappoint. Detailed, expert
knowledge of both properties

and areas is offered and "what we don't know, we'll find out". The minimum service offered is the property rental only, but air (charter or scheduled) or ferry-inclusive arrangements, car hire etc are available just as the client requires. Quality also defines both style and location of accommodation which varies from classic restored masias or farmhouses to modern villas, all with private pools. We offer the widest range of country houses with pools in Catalonia, concentrating in the Girona province, parts where the local culture is strong and close to its dramatic, unspoilt coastline. We also feature houses with pools in rural Majorca, in the mountainous north and by the sleepy, agricultural villages of the south-east. Their tranquil settings, but proximity to the coast mean that our houses are ideal for family holidays.'

Self-catering holidays:
Catalonia, Balearic Islands

Waymark Holidays
44 Windsor Road,
Slough SL1 2EJ
Admin: 0753 516477
Res: 0753 516477
Fax: 0753 517016
ATOL: 624
Visa, Access
'Waymark is a specialist in walking and cross-country skiing holidays. The walks are graded from easy to strenuous. Holidays are either centre-based or tours – hotel to hotel or hut to hut. The groups are small and are all accompanied by experienced leaders. Waymark has been operating since 1973 and takes around 2400 walking clients abroad each year. In Spain only walking holidays are offered and our destinations include the Pyrenees, Galicia, Alicante, Andalucia and the Picos de Europa.'
Special interest holidays:
Walking and trekking

Other titles in this series by Frank Barrett:

Family France

Family USA

Family Italy